T0054963

Little Oxford Dictionary of
Proverbs

Little Oxford Dictionary of

Proverbs

SECOND EDITION

Edited by
Elizabeth Knowles

OXFORD
UNIVERSITY PRESS

Great Clarendon Street, Oxford, OX2 6DP,
United Kingdom

Oxford University Press is a department of the University of Oxford.
It furthers the University's objective of excellence in research, scholarship,
and education by publishing worldwide. Oxford is a registered trade mark of
Oxford University Press in the UK and in certain other countries

First Edition published in 2009
Second Edition published in 2016

Impression: 2

Published in the United States of America by Oxford University Press
198 Madison Avenue, New York, NY 10016, United States of America

British Library Cataloguing in Publication Data

Data available

Library of Congress Control Number: 2016943803

ISBN 978-0-19-877837-0

Printed in India by
Replika Press Pvt. Ltd.

 # Contents

Introduction ❧

This new edition of the *Little Oxford Dictionary of Proverbs* once more brings together a wide range of proverbs and sayings, from the traditional Western maxims of biblical and classical tradition, through proverbs from across the wider world, to expressions of contemporary wisdom from popular culture. The selection made is based on the diversity of real usage: when reaching today for a saying to use in advice or admonition, we happily draw material from a broad range of sources. New additions from today's world include the advice to interviewees to 'Dress for the job you want, not for the job you have', and the rueful reflection from the world of computing that in matters of online security, 'There is no patch for stupid.'

The dictionary is arranged by theme, so that a number of sayings on each topic can be found together. Subjects covered range widely, from **Action** ('The shrimp that falls asleep is swept away by the current') to **Cooperation** ('Cross the river in a crowd and the crocodile won't eat you'), and from **Friendship** ('The road to a friend's house is never long') to **Gardens** ('A garden is never finished'). A piece of advice for **Parents** may resonate with anyone seeing a son or daughter off on a gap year: 'Send the beloved child on a journey.' Within each theme, the proverbs and sayings are arranged alphabetically (initial 'a' and 'the' being ignored). There is a keyword index for essential words from the first part of each saying, allowing the reader to trace a saying to its place in its particular theme.

One of the pleasures of proverbs is in seeing how, in different parts of the world, the same idea may be expressed.

Introduction

At **Optimism and Pessimism**, the traditional rueful reflection that 'If wishes were horses, beggars would ride' is now matched by a comment from Senegal: 'If you had teeth of steel, you could eat iron coconuts.' Under **Power**, the reflection from Africa that 'When elephants fight, it is the grass that gets hurt' is echoed by the Korean saying 'When whales fight, the shrimp's back is broken.'

At **Caution**, the traditional English adjuration to 'Look before you leap' is now reinforced by a Chinese saying recommending a different form of careful exploration, 'Cross the river by feeling the stones.' 'Be what you want to seem' at **Behaviour** finds an echo in the more recent, 'Fake it 'til you make it.'

Sometimes, of course, different approaches are emphasized. At **Ability**, the idea that someone not naturally suited to a task will perform poorly is traditionally expressed by the proverb 'A sow may whistle, though it has an ill mouth for it.' The African saying 'If you can talk, you can sing, and if you can walk, you can dance' offers a much more positive approach. Views of **Enemies** range from 'The enemy of my enemy is my friend' to the warning 'Do not call a wolf to help you against the dogs.' The section on **Crises** includes two divergent modern contributions: the advice to 'Keep calm and carry on', and the wryer comment, 'Never waste a good crisis.'

Some new items have come to attention through high profile use. Hillary Clinton, speaking at a fundraising dinner in Arkansas when running for the Democratic nomination, used the saying 'If you see a turtle on a fencepost, it didn't get there by accident': this has now been added to **Causes and Consequences**. President Michael Higgins of Ireland, thanking those who had given help to

Introduction

the injured after the collapse of a balcony in Berkeley had resulted in the death and injury of a number of Irish students, quoted the Irish saying, 'We live in each other's shadow'. This now appears at **Cooperation.** At times, a news item may unexpectedly put us in touch with another culture. In October 2015, news from the British bird reserve of Slimbridge about the annual arrival of whooper swans quoted a Russian proverb associating migrating swans with impending wintry weather: 'The swan brings snow on its bill' (this is now at **Birds**).

One of the fascinating things about language is that we can never really say with certainty that a maxim which has fallen out of use may not reappear. The traditional saying 'A wise man turns chance into good fortune' seemed to have dropped out of use. However, when in November 2015 President Xi Jinping of China was entertained at a Buckingham Palace state banquet, he included it in his speech as a famous British adage. The proverb is now to be found at **Opportunity**.

An Arab proverb advises, 'To understand the people, acquaint yourself with their proverbs'. Working on this book has again been particularly pleasurable because of the opportunity to observe a multiplicity of views, and to enjoy the vigour and creativity of language. I hope that once more some of this pleasure will be shared with the reader.

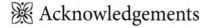 Acknowledgements

Little Proverbs has once more drawn on the most recent
editions of the *Oxford Treasury of Sayings & Quotations*
(4/e, 2011) and the *Oxford Dictionary of Proverbs* (6/e, 2015).
This material has been augmented by Oxford's Quotations
reading programme, the Oxford Corpus, and the Editor's
own reading and research. Any book of this kind rests
on the research, scholarship, and insight of many others,
and I am extremely fortunate to have had such a foundation.
I am grateful too to Ben Harris, who had the original idea
for this book, and to Joanna Harris and Susan Ratcliffe who
have provided valuable editorial support.

ELIZABETH KNOWLES
Oxford 2016

List of Subjects �֎

List of Subjects

List of Subjects

List of Subjects

Ability

The consensus of proverbial wisdom is that ability (or the lack of it) is innate, although aptitudes may be developed: If you can talk, you can sing; if you can walk, you can dance.

Genius is an infinite capacity for taking pains.
English proverb, late 19th century.

Horses for courses.
originally (in horse-racing) meaning that different horses are suited to different racecourses, but now used more generally to mean that different people are suited to different roles; English proverb, late 19th century.

If you can talk, you can sing; if you can walk, you can dance.
often used as an encouragement to undertake something new; African (Shona) proverb.

Inside the forest there are many birds.
people are of many different kinds and abilities ('many birds' here = 'birds of many kinds'); Chinese proverb.

Is Saul also among the prophets?
a rhetorical question asked when someone displays unexpected abilities; from the biblical account (1 Samuel 10:11), in which the young Saul's prophesying became one of the signs that he had been chosen as king of Israel.

Absence

A sow may whistle, though it has an ill mouth for it.
someone not naturally suited to a task will perform it badly;
English proverb, early 19th century.

Absence

See also MEETING AND PARTING

Despite the saying that Absence makes the heart
grow fonder, *it is possible that an absent person who
is not present to defend themselves may be blamed for
something, or simply forgotten.*

Absence is the mother of disillusion.
American proverb, mid 20th century.

Absence makes the heart grow fonder.
affection for a person is strengthened by missing them;
English proverb, mid 19th century, derived from a Latin
proverb recorded from the 1st century BC.

Absence of evidence is not evidence of absence.
traditional saying, recorded from the 19th century.

The absent get farther away every day.
Japanese proverb.

He who is absent is always in the wrong.
someone who is not present cannot defend themselves;
English proverb, mid 15th century.

A little absence does much good.

American proverb, mid 20th century.

Out of sight, out of mind.

someone who is not present is easily forgotten; English
proverb, mid 13th century.

Achievement

See also AMBITION, EFFORT, PROBLEMS AND SOLUTIONS,
SUCCESS AND FAILURE

*Effort and aspiration are both needed for achievement,
but even if the goal is reached the outcome may
not be satisfactory, since* While the grass grows,
the steed starves.

Behind an able man there are other able men.

modern saying, said to be a Chinese proverb.

The difficult is done at once.

slogan of the US Armed Forces; recorded earlier as a
comment by the French statesman Charles Alexandre
de Calonne (1734–1802), 'Madam, if a thing is possible,
consider it done; the impossible?—that will be done.'

**The hand will not reach what the heart does not
long for.**

desire is essential for achievement; Welsh proverb.

Achievement

He who likes cherries soon learns to climb.
achievement seen as the result of motivation;
German proverb.

In a calm sea every man is a pilot.
apparent achievement may not have been tested by
circumstances; English proverb, recorded from the early
19th century.

***Palmam qui meruit, ferat* [Let him who has won it bear the palm].**
Latin, adopted by Lord Nelson (1758–1805) as his motto,
from John Jortin *Lusus Poetici* (3rd ed., 1748), 'Ad Ventos'.

***Per ardua ad astra* [Through struggle to the stars].**
Latin, motto of the Mulvany family, quoted and translated
by Rider Haggard in his novel *The People of the Mist* (1894),
and still in use as a motto of the Royal Air Force, having
been approved by King George V in 1913.

Seekers are finders.
success is the result of effort; Persian proverb; compare **Seek
and ye shall find** at ACTION AND INACTION.

Still achieving, still pursuing.
American proverb, mid 20th century, from Henry
Wadsworth Longfellow's adjuration, 'Let us, then, be up
and doing, With a heart for any fate; Still achieving, still

pursuing, Learn to labour and to wait' from the poem
'A Psalm of Life' (1838).

Whatever man has done, man can do.
anything that has been achieved once can be achieved again;
English proverb, mid 14th century.

While the grass grows, the steed starves.
by the time hopes or expectations can be satisfied, it may be
too late; English proverb, mid 14th century.

You cannot have your cake and eat it.
you cannot have things both ways; English proverb, mid
16th century.

Action and Inaction

See also IDLENESS, WORDS AND DEEDS

*While setting out on a planned course is likely to be
rewarded, since we are told that* Seek and ye shall find,
there are also dangers in not thinking things through:
Action without thought is shooting without aim.

Action is worry's worst enemy.
advocating the control of fruitless worry by taking a
decision and acting upon it; American proverb, mid
20th century.

Action and Inaction

Action this day.
annotation as used by Winston Churchill at the Admiralty
in 1940.

Action without thought is shooting without aim.
American proverb, mid 20th century.

A barking dog never bites.
noisy threats often do not presage real danger; English
proverb, 16th century; recorded earlier in French in the
13th century.

**Better to light one candle than to curse the
darkness.**
motto of the American Christopher Society, founded
in 1945.

If it ain't broke, don't fix it.
warning against interference with something that is working
satisfactorily; late 20th-century saying.

If you want something done, ask a busy person.
implying that a busy person is most likely to have
learned how to manage their time efficiently; late 20th
century saying.

It is as cheap sitting as standing.
often used literally; English proverb, mid 17th century.

Action and Inaction

Lookers-on see most of the game.
those who are not participating are able to take an overall view; English proverb, early 16th century.

The road to hell is paved with good intentions.
often used as a comment on well-intentioned actions that have turned out badly; English proverb, late 16th century (earlier forms omit the first three words).

Seek and ye shall find.
an active search for something wanted is likely to be rewarded; English proverb, mid 16th century, from the Bible (Matthew 7:7), 'Ask, and it shall be given you: seek, and ye shall find'; compare **Seekers are finders** at ACHIEVEMENT.

The shrimp that falls asleep is swept away by the current.
if you get distracted you will fall behind; Spanish proverb, *Camarón que se duerme se lo lleva la corriente.*

When in doubt, do nowt.
advising against taking action when one is unsure of one's ground; English proverb, mid 19th century.

Adversity

See also MISFORTUNES, SUFFERING

*Adversity is unavoidable, and may in fact be salutary;
a modern saying advises making the best of it*: If life
hands you lemons, make lemonade. *We also, according
at least to a Swahili proverb, have the comfort that
adversity is finite:* After hardship comes relief.

Adversity introduces a man to himself.

modern saying, implying that experiencing difficult
circumstances leads to self-knowledge.

Adversity is the foundation of virtue.

Japanese proverb.

Adversity makes strange bedfellows.

shared difficulties may bring together very different people;
English proverb, mid 19th century.

After hardship comes relief.

African proverb (Swahili).

A dose of adversity is often as needful as a dose
of medicine.

American proverb, mid 20th century.

If life hands you lemons, make lemonade.

an adjuration to make the best of difficult circumstances;
late 20th century saying.

Advertising

It is tempting to think of advertising as a modern phenomenon, but the awareness that It pays to advertise *goes back a considerable way, as* Good wine needs no bush *shows.*

Any publicity is good publicity.
it is always preferable to have attention focused on a name than to be unnoticed; English proverb, early 20th century.

Blow your own horn, even if you don't sell a clam.
American saying.

Don't advertise what you can't fulfil.
American proverb, mid 20th century.

Good wine needs no bush.
there is no need to advertise or boast about something of good quality as people will always discover its merits, referring to the bunch of ivy that was formerly the sign of a vintner's shop; English proverb, early 15th century.

It pays to advertise.
American proverb, mid 20th century.

Let's run it up the flagpole and see if anyone salutes it.
recorded as an established expression in the 1960s, suggesting the testing of a new idea or product.

Advice

Caution should be exercised in the giving and receiving of advice: against the warning Don't teach your grandmother to suck eggs, *we have the reminder that* A fool may give a wise man counsel.

Ask advice, but use your common sense.
American proverb, mid 20th century.

Don't teach your grandmother to suck eggs.
a caution against offering advice to the wise and experienced; English proverb, early 18th century.

A fool may give a wise man counsel.
sometimes used as a warning against overconfidence in one's judgement; English proverb, mid 14th century.

Never give advice unless asked.
German proverb.

Night brings counsel.
sometimes used as a warning against overconfidence in one's judgement; English proverb, mid 14th century.

A nod's as good as a wink to a blind horse.
the slightest hint is enough to convey one's meaning in a particular case; English proverb, late 18th century.

A word to the wise is enough.

only a very brief warning is necessary to an intelligent person; English proverb, early 16th century; earlier in Latin *'verbum sat sapienti* [a word is sufficient to a wise man]'.

Age

See also YOUTH

The consensus on the latter part of life is that experience is likely to have brought wisdom: the 'fool at forty' is an exception to the view that The older the ginger the more pungent its flavour.

Age is just a number.

modern saying.

A fool at forty is a fool indeed.

someone who has not learned wisdom by the age of forty will never learn it; in this form from Edward Young's *Universal Passions* (1725), 'Be wise with speed; A fool at forty is a fool indeed'; English proverb, early 16th century.

For the unlearned, old age is winter; for the learned, it is the season of harvest.

Jewish saying.

Age

The fox may grow grey, but never good.

ageing will not change a person's essential nature; English proverb; compare **The wolf may lose his teeth, but never his nature** below.

The gods send nuts to those who have no teeth.

opportunities or pleasures often come too late to be enjoyed; English proverb, early 20th century.

Life begins at forty.

English proverb, mid 20th century, from the title of a book (1932) by Walter B. Pitkin.

Like fine wine,—gets better with age.

modern saying.

The older the ginger the more pungent its flavour.

older people have more knowledge and experience than the young; Chinese proverb.

An old horse does not spoil the furrow.

Russian proverb; compare **There's many a good tune played on an old fiddle** below.

There's many a good tune played on an old fiddle.

someone's abilities do not depend on their being young; English proverb, early 20th century; compare **An old horse does not spoil the furrow** above.

There's no fool like an old fool.

often used to suggest that folly in an older person, who should be wiser, is particularly acute; English proverb, mid 16th century.

When an elder dies, it is as if a whole library has burned down.

African proverb.

The wolf may lose his teeth, but never his nature.

age may affect physical strength, but not a dangerous nature; English proverb; compare **The fox may grow grey, but never good** above.

Ambition

See also ACHIEVEMENT, SUCCESS AND FAILURE

Although There is always room at the top *is encouraging, proverbial wisdom warns that the results of pursuing one's goals may be less than happy:* Many go out for wool and come home shorn.

Aut Caesar, aut nihil [Caesar or nothing].

motto coined by Cesare Borgia (1476–1507), and inscribed on his sword.

Ambition

Hasty climbers have sudden falls.

the over-ambitious often fail to take necessary precautions;
English proverb, mid 15th century.

The higher the monkey climbs the more he shows his tail.

the further an unsuitable person is advanced, the more their
inadequacies are apparent; English proverb, late 14th century.

It's ill waiting for dead men's shoes.

often used of a situation in which one is hoping for a
position currently occupied by another; English proverb,
mid 16th century; compare **A bloody war and a sickly
season** at ARMED FORCES.

Many go out for wool and come home shorn.

many who seek to better themselves or make themselves
rich end by losing what they already have; English proverb,
late 16th century.

The smaller the lizard, the greater its hopes of becoming a crocodile.

lack of power may be a spur to ambition; African proverb.

There is always room at the top.

as a response to being advised against joining the
overcrowded legal profession, it is also attributed to the
American politician and lawyer Daniel Webster (1782–1852);
English proverb, early 20th century.

Anger

Losing your temper is unproductive, since Anger
improves nothing but the arch of a cat's back;
*traditional advice suggests using soft answers to deflect
the anger of others, and counting to a hundred to avoid
becoming angry yourself.*

Anger improves nothing but the arch of a cat's back.
American proverb, mid 20th century.

**He that will be angry for anything will be angry
for nothing.**
frequent anger is likely to be prompted by petty reasons;
Scottish proverb.

A little pot is soon hot.
a small person soon becomes angry or passionate; English
proverb, mid 16th century.

A soft answer turneth away wrath.
with allusion to the Bible (Proverbs 15:1); English proverb,
late Middle English.

When angry count a hundred.
advising against precipitate response (the number proposed
varies, and sometimes the advice is '…recite the alphabet');
English proverb, late 16th century.

Apology and Excuses

Making excuses to avoid blame is regarded poorly, since He who excuses himself, accuses himself, *and we are told that* A bad workman blames his tools. *However, it may be right to try to make some kind of explanation:* A bad excuse is better than none.

Apology is only egoism wrong side out.

American proverb, mid 20th century.

A bad excuse is better than none.

It is better to attempt to give some kind of explanation, even a weak one; English proverb, mid 16th century.

A bad workman blames his tools.

often used as a comment on someone's excuses for their lack of success; English proverb, early 17th century, late 13th century in French; (compare **One who cannot dance blames the uneven floor** at DANCE).

Don't make excuses, make good.

American proverb, mid 20th century.

He who excuses himself, accuses himself.

often used to mean that attempts to excuse oneself show a guilty conscience; English proverb, early 17th century.

It is easy to find a stick to beat a dog.
it is easy to find reasons to criticize someone who is
vulnerable; English proverb, mid 16th century.

When you are in a hole, stop digging.
complicated explanations and attempts to exculpate
oneself often make a bad situation worse; late 20th century
saying; often associated with the British Labour politician
Denis Healey.

Appearance

See also BEAUTY, THE BODY

The idea that Appearances are deceptive *is reflected
in a number of sayings. While it may be true that* A
carpenter is known by his chips, *we are cautioned in a
number of ways against judging by the outward look.*

Appearances are deceptive.
the outward form of something may not be a true guide to
its real nature; English proverb, mid 17th century.

A blind man's wife needs no paint.
there is no point in making efforts that cannot be appreciated;
English proverb, mid 17th century.

Appearance

A carpenter is known by his chips.
the nature of a person's occupation or interest is demonstrated by the traces left behind; English proverb, mid 16th century.

The cowl does not make the monk.
warning against judging nature and moral character by appearance; English proverb, late 14th century.

Distance lends enchantment to the view.
English proverb, late 18th century, from the lines ''Tis distance lends enchantment to the view, and robes the mountain in its azure hue', by Thomas Campbell (1777–1844) in *Pleasures of Hope* (1799).

Do not judge a tree by its bark.
a warning against making assumptions based on the outward appearance; Italian proverb.

A fair skin hides seven defects.
Japanese proverb; compare **Beauty is only skin deep** at BEAUTY.

A good horse cannot be of a bad colour.
colour is not an indicator of a horse's quality; English proverb, early 17th century.

A man without culture is like a zebra without stripes.
African proverb (Masai).

Merit in appearance is more rewarded than merit itself.

American proverb, mid 20th century.

Never choose your women or linen by candlelight.

warning against being deceived by apparent attractions seen in a poor light; English proverb, late 16th century.

What you see is what you get.

used generally to mean that the function and value of something can be deduced from its outward appearance, and that there are no hidden drawbacks or advantages; late 20th century computing expression, from which the acronym *wysiwig* derives.

You can't tell a book by its cover.

outward appearance is not a guide to a person's real nature; English proverb, early 20th century.

Architecture

Building is likely to involve expense, although the 17th-century view that Building and marrying of children are great wasters *may be thought too severe.*

The arch never sleeps.

saying, meaning that an arch constantly thrusts against keystone and walls.

Architecture

Building and marrying of children are great wasters.
comparing two major sources of expense for the head of a household; English proverb.

In settling an island, the first building erected by a Spaniard will be a church; by a Frenchman, a fort; by a Dutchman, a warehouse; and by an Englishman, an alehouse.
English proverb, late 18th century.

It is easier to build two chimneys than to maintain one.
the cost of using and maintaining a building may be much greater than the cost of building it; English proverb, mid 16th century.

No good building without a good foundation.
English proverb, late 15th century.

***Si monumentum requiris, circumspice* [If you seek a monument, gaze around].**
Latin inscription in St Paul's Cathedral, London, applied to Sir Christopher Wren, its architect, and attributed to Wren's son.

Argument

See also OPINION

Positive injunctions to avoid quarrelling, such as
Birds in their little nests agree, *are reinforced by*
pragmatic reflections as to the dangers of indulging in
disagreement: While two dogs are fighting for a bone,
a third runs away with it.

Birds in their little nests agree.

used as a direction that young children should not argue
among themselves; a nursery proverb from Isaac Watts
Divine Songs (1715).

Do not argue against the sun.

there is no point in disputing what is obvious; saying, of
Latin origin.

It takes two to make a quarrel.

some responsibility for a disagreement rests with each party
to it; English proverb, early 18th century.

The more arguments you win, the less friends you will have.

American proverb, mid 20th century.

The only thing a heated argument ever produced is coolness.

American proverb, mid 20th century.

The Armed Forces

While two dogs are fighting for a bone, a third runs away with it.
while the attention of two disputants is on their quarrel, they may lose possession of what they are fighting over to a third party; English proverb, late 14th century, which gave rise to the phrase 'bone of contention'.

✺ The Armed Forces
See also WARFARE

A number of sayings reflect life within the armed forces over several centuries, from the naval toast A bloody war and a sickly season from the time of the Napoleonic wars, to the advice to soldiers in the Second World War: If it moves, salute it; if it doesn't move, pick it up; and if you can't pick it up, paint it.

The army knows how to gain a victory but not how to make proper use of it.
American proverb, mid 20th century.

An army of stags led by a lion would be more formidable than one of lions led by a stag.
courage and tenacity can be negated by poor leadership, while a strong leader can provide crucial encouragement for weak forces; English military saying, of classical origin.

The Armed Forces

A bloody war and a sickly season.

naval toast in the time of Nelson, when an increased death rate meant more rapid promotion; compare **It's ill waiting for dead men's shoes** at AMBITION and **a willing foe and sea room** below.

The first duty of a soldier is obedience.

English proverb, mid 19th century.

If it moves, salute it; if it doesn't move, pick it up; and if you can't pick it up, paint it.

1940s military saying.

Old soldiers never die.

English proverb, early 20th century.

Providence is always on the side of the big battalions.

English proverb, early 19th century; a similar thought can be found earlier in other languages, as the words of the Roman senator and historian Tacitus, 'Deos fortioribus adesse [The gods are on the side of the stronger]', and the comment in a letter of the French soldier and poet the Comte de Bussy Rabutin (1618–93), 'As you know, God is usually on the side of the big squadrons against the small.'

A singing army and a singing people can't be defeated.

American proverb, mid 20th century.

Art

A soldier of the Great War known unto God.
adopted by the War Graves Commission as the standard epitaph for the unidentified dead of the First World War.

A willing foe and sea room.
naval toast in the time of Nelson (compare **a bloody war and a sickly season** above).

Your King and Country need you.
1914 recruiting advertisement, showing Lord Kitchener with pointing finger.

Your soul may belong to God, but your ass belongs to the army.
American saying to new recruits, mid 20th century.

 # Art

Even a talented painter needs to practise their art: the advice Not a day without a line *goes back to the classical world.*

Every painter paints himself.
Italian proverb, said to be of Renaissance origin.

A good painter can draw a devil as well as an angel.
English proverb, late 16th century.

Not a day without a line.
traditional saying, attributed to the Greek artist Apelles (fl. 325 BC) by Pliny the Elder.

Autumn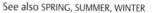

See also SPRING, SUMMER, WINTER

There are notably fewer proverbs about Autumn than the other seasons, and those in use today sound a cautionary note.

All autumns do not fill granaries.
Estonian proverb.

Chickens are counted in the autumn.
Russian proverb; compare **Don't count your chickens before they are hatched** at OPTIMISM, and **May chickens come cheeping** at SPRING.

If you do not sow in the spring, you will not reap in the autumn.
Irish proverb.

September blow soft till the fruit's in the loft.
expressing the hope that fine weather often customary in September will hold until a crop of apples or other fruit has been picked and stored; English proverb, late 16th century.

September dries up wells or breaks down bridges.
traditional saying, suggesting that September can see either drought or flood.

Beauty

See also APPEARANCE, THE BODY

The early 20th-century advertising slogan Beauty is power *reflects a traditional awareness of the force of physical attraction, but as far back as the 17th century we have also been warned that* Beauty is only skin deep.

Beauty draws with a single hair.

asserting the powerful attraction of a woman's beauty (often shown as outdoing great physical strength); English proverb, late 16th century.

Beauty is a good letter of introduction.

American proverb, mid 20th century.

Beauty is in the eye of the beholder.

beauty is not judged objectively, but according to the beholder's estimation; English proverb, early 17th century.

Beauty is only skin deep.

physical beauty is no guarantee of a good character or temperament; English proverb, early 17th century; compare **A fair skin hides seven defects** at APPEARANCE.

Beauty is power.

advertising slogan for Helena Rubinstein's Valaze Skin Food, 1904.

Black is beautiful.

slogan of American civil rights campaigners, mid 1960s.

It is the beautiful bird that gets caged.

beauty has its own dangers; Chinese proverb.

Monday's child is fair of face.

first line of a traditional rhyme, mid 19th century (compare qualities associated with birth on other days at entries under GIFTS, SORROW, TRAVEL, and WORK).

Please your eye and plague your heart.

contrasting the pleasure given by the appearance of a beautiful person with the heartache they may cause; English proverb, early 17th century.

The prettiest girl in the world can only give what she has.

French proverb, *La plus belle fille du monde ne peut donner que ce qu'elle a.*

Beginning

See also CHANGE, ENDING

Starting well is important, as we are told that A good beginning makes a good ending, *but it is also wise to consider whether the course on which you are embarking is a wise one:* It is easier to raise the Devil than to lay him.

Beginning

Beginning is easy; continuing is hard.
a good start is not enough, since success requires
pertinacity; modern saying, said to be a Japanese proverb.

First impressions are the most lasting.
English proverb, early 18th century.

The golden rule of life is, make a beginning.
American proverb, mid 20th century.

A good beginning makes a good ending.
getting things right at the outset is likely to ensure success;
English proverb, early 14th century.

It is easier to raise the Devil than to lay him.
sometimes used to mean that it is easier to start a process
than to stop it; English proverb, mid 17th century.

It is the first step that is difficult.
English proverb, late 16th century.

The longest journey begins with a single step.
often used to emphasize how important a single decision
may be; late 20th-century saying, ultimately derived from
words of the Chinese philosopher Lao Tzu (*c*.604–*c*.531 BC)
in the *Tao-te Ching*, 'A tower of nine storeys begins with a
heap of earth. The journey of a thousand *li* starts from
where one stands.'

The sooner begun, the sooner done.

used as a warning against putting off a necessary but
unwanted task; English proverb, late 16th century.

There is always a first time.

English proverb, late 16th century.

Well begun is half done.

emphasizing the importance of a successful beginning
to the completion of a project; English proverb, early
15th century.

Behaviour

See also MANNERS, WORDS AND DEEDS

*While there is a traditional emphasis on the importance
of right action, as in* Do as I say, not as I do, *there is
also a certain scepticism about what may be only the
appearance of good behaviour:* Handsome is as
handsome does.

Be what you would seem to be.

English proverb, late 14th century; earlier in classical
sources, as in *Seven against Thebes* by the Greek tragedian
Aeschylus (*c*.525–456 BC), 'He wishes not to appear but to
be the best.'

Behaviour

By a sweet tongue and kindness, you can drag an elephant by a hair.
Middle Eastern proverb, commonly found in this form in Arabic; the equivalent proverb in Persian has 'drag a snake'.

Cleanliness is next to godliness.
next here means 'immediately following', as in serial order, and is now often used humorously to mean 'the second most desirable quality possible'; English proverb, late 18th century.

Do as I say, not as I do.
often used with an imputation of hypocrisy; English proverb, mid 16th century.

Evil communications corrupt good manners.
proper conduct is harmfully influenced by false information or knowledge; the saying is also sued to assert the deleterious effect of bad example; English proverb, early 15th century, from the Bible (1 Corinthians 15:33).

Fake it 'til you make it.
self-help motto from the 1970s, now often associated with Alcoholics Anonymous.

Good behaviour is the last refuge of mediocrity.
American proverb, mid 20th century.

Handsome is as handsome does.

handsome here referred to chivalrous or genteel behaviour, although it is often popularly taken to refer to good looks; English proverb, late 16th century; compare **Pretty is as pretty does** below.

He is a good dog who goes to church.

good character is shown by moral custom and practice; English proverb, early 19th century.

It is one thing to keep your morals on high plane; it's another to keep up with them.

American proverb, mid 20th century.

Never do evil that good may come of it.

the prospect of a good outcome cannot justify wrongdoing; English proverb, late 16th century.

Pretty is as pretty does.

American proverb, mid 19th century, equivalent of **Handsome is as handsome does** above.

When in Rome, do as the Romans do.

English proverb, late 15th century; ultimately deriving from a passage in a letter of St Ambrose, AD *c*.400, 'When I go to Rome, I fast on Saturday, but here [Milan] I do not. Do you also follow the custom of whatever church you attend, if you do not want to give or receive scandal.'

Belief

See also CERTAINTY AND DOUBT

Belief may relate to religious faith as in Faith will move mountains, *but some traditional sayings deal with more general questions of how you should approach the world around you:* Believe nothing of what you hear, and only half of what you see.

Believe nothing of what you hear, and only half of what you see.
English proverb, mid 19th century; a related Middle English saying warns that you should not believe everything that is said or that you hear.

A believer is a songless bird in a cage.
American proverb, late 19th century.

Believing has a core of unbelieving.
American proverb, mid 19th century.

Don't strain at a gnat, and swallow a camel.
do not make difficulties over a small matter, when you have already accepted something of much greater importance; saying with biblical allusion, to Matthew 23:24, 'Ye blind guides, which strain at a gnat, and swallow a camel.'

Faith will move mountains.

with the help of faith something naturally impossible can be achieved; English proverb, late 19th century, in allusion to the Bible (Matthew 17:20, 'If ye have faith as a grain of mustard seed, ye shall say unto this mountain, Remove hence to yonder place; and it shall remove').

Pigs may fly, but they are very unlikely birds.

English proverb, mid 19th century.

Seeing is believing.

acceptance of the existence of something depends on actual demonstration; English proverb, early 17th century.

Birds

Sayings relating to birds are likely to reflect the associations of particular species, from the English magpies whose gathering may foretell sorrow or mirth, to the rare white heron of New Zealand.

Birds of prey do not sing.

German proverb.

The cuckoo comes in April, He sings his song in May; In the middle of June He changes his tune, And then he flies away.

traditional rhyme.

Birds

A mockingbird has no voice of his own.

the mockingbird is known for its mimicry of the calls and songs of other birds; American proverb, mid 19th century.

One for sorrow; two for mirth; three for a wedding, four for a birth.

a traditional rhyme found in a variety of forms, referring to the number of magpies seen on a particular occasion; English proverb, mid 19th century.

The robin and the wren are God's cock and hen; the martin and the swallow are God's mate and marrow.

there was a traditional belief that the robin and the wren were sacred birds, and that to harm them in any way would be unlucky (*marrow* = 'companion'); English proverb, late 18th century.

The swan brings snow on its bill.

the arrival of migrating swans may be the harbinger of wintry weather; Russian proverb.

The white heron is a bird of a single flight.

the white heron is very rare; Maori proverb.

The Body

See also APPEARANCE, BEAUTY, THE SENSES

Physical characteristics may give a clue to inner qualities, from Cold hands, warm heart *to* The larger the body, the bigger the heart.

Cold hands, warm heart.

an outward sign may contradict an inward reality; English proverb, early 20th century.

The eyes are the window of the soul.

it is in the eyes that a person's true nature may be discerned; English proverb, mid 16th century.

The larger the body, the bigger the heart.

American proverb, mid 20th century.

Books

See also READING, WRITING

While not every book is admirable (A great book is a great evil), *the consensus of proverbial wisdom is in favour of the written word:* A book is like a garden carried in the pocket.

Borrowing

Beware of the man of one book.
warning against the person who places too much
confidence in a single authority; Latin proverb.

A book is like a garden carried in the pocket.
Middle Eastern saying.

A great book is a great evil.
a long book is likely to be verbose and badly written;
English proverb, early 17th century; a contraction of
Callimachus (*c.*305–*c.*240 BC), 'The great book is equal
to a great evil.'

A library is a repository of medicine for the mind.
American proverb, mid 20th century.

 # Borrowing
See DEBT AND BORROWING

 # British Towns and Regions
*Local pride is an enduring quality, whether expressed in
a traditional saying such as* Kirton was a borough
town when Exon was a vuzzy down, *or a 20th-century
slogan such as* Glasgow's miles better.

Essex stiles, Kentish miles, Norfolk wiles, many a man beguiles.

traditional saying, early 17th century.

From Hell, Hull, and Halifax, good Lord deliver us.

traditional saying, late 16th century.

Glasgow's miles better.

slogan introduced by Provost Michael Kelly, 1980s.

Kirton was a borough town when Exon was a vuzzy down.

on the relative ages of Crediton (*Kirton*) and Exeter (*Exon*); traditional saying.

Lincoln was, London is, and York shall be.

referring to which is the greatest city; traditional saying, late 16th century.

May God in His mercy look down on Belfast.

traditional refrain.

Northamptonshire for squires and spires.

traditional saying, late 19th century.

Peebles for pleasure.

the town of Peebles in the Scottish Borders has traditionally been a favoured holiday resort; traditional saying, late 19th century.

British Towns and Regions

Some places of Kent have health and no wealth, some wealth and no health, some health and wealth.

referring to the north and east part of the county, Romney Marsh, and the Weald respectively; traditional saying, late 16th century.

Sussex won't be druv.

asserting that Sussex people have minds of their own, and cannot be forced against their will (*druv* is a dialect version of *drove*, meaning *driven*); English proverb, early 20th century.

Take away Aberdeen and twelve miles round, and where are you?

Scottish saying, reflecting local pride in the city.

There are more saints in Cornwall than in heaven.

traditional saying, relating to the number of West Country saints known through their local cult.

What Manchester says today, the rest of England says tomorrow.

English proverb, late 19th century, occurring in a variety of forms.

Yorkshire born and Yorkshire bred, strong in the arm and weak in the head.

the names of other (chiefly northern) English counties and towns are also used instead of Yorkshire; English proverb, mid 19th century.

Broadcasting

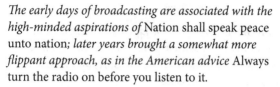

The early days of broadcasting are associated with the high-minded aspirations of Nation shall speak peace unto nation; *later years brought a somewhat more flippant approach, as in the American advice* Always turn the radio on before you listen to it.

Always turn the radio on before you listen to it.
American saying, mid 20th century.

Assistant heads must roll!
traditional solution to management problems
in broadcasting.

Nation shall speak peace unto nation.
motto of the BBC, adapted from the Bible (Isaiah 2:4,
'Nation shall not lift up sword against nation, neither
shall they learn war any more') by Montague John
Rendall (1862–1950).

To inform, educate, and entertain.
traditional expression of the mission of the BBC, associated
with Lord Reith (1889–1971).

Business

See also BUYING AND SELLING

While not all sayings go as far as the modern Business
is war, *there is a consensus in favour of determined
application:* Business before pleasure, *and* Business
neglected is business lost.

Bull markets climb a wall of worry.

signs of recovery from a recession are treated with
scepticism; modern saying.

Business before pleasure.

often used to encourage a course of action; English proverb,
mid 19th century.

Business goes where it is invited and stays where it is well treated.

American proverb, mid 20th century.

Business is like a car: it will not run by itself except downhill.

American proverb, mid 20th century.

Business is war.

modern saying, sometimes said to be of Japanese origin.

Business neglected is business lost.

North American proverb, mid 20th century.

The customer is always right.

English proverb, early 20th century; compare a saying of the
Swiss hotel proprietor César Ritz (1850–1918), *'Le client n'a
jamais tort* [The customer is never wrong].'

He that cannot abide a bad market does not deserve a good one.

to be successful in business you must be able to deal
with bad times as well as good; English proverb, late
17th century.

If you don't speculate, you can't accumulate.

outlay (and some degree of risk) is necessary if real gain is
to be achieved; English proverb, mid 20th century.

Keep your own shop and your shop will keep you.

recommending attention to what is essential to one's
livelihood; English proverb, early 17th century.

Never try to catch a falling knife.

do not invest in a failing business; figurative use of health
and safety advice for caterers.

No cure, no pay.

known principally from its use on Lloyd's of London's
Standard Form of Salvage Agreement; English proverb,
late 19th century.

Buying and Selling

No penny, no paternoster.

if you want a thing you must pay for it (the allusion is to priests insisting on being paid for performing services); English proverb, late 16th century.

Pay beforehand was never well served.

payment in advance removes the incentive to finish the work; English proverb, late 16th century.

Pile it high, sell it cheap.

slogan coined by Jack Cohen (1898–1979), founder of the Tesco supermarket chain.

There are tricks in every trade.

the practice of every skill is likely to involve some trickery or dishonesty; English proverb, mid 17th century.

Trade follows the flag.

commercial development is likely to follow military intervention; English proverb, late 19th century.

✵ Buying and Selling

See also BUSINESS

The warning Let the buyer beware, *drawn ultimately from the classical world, enshrines a core belief about the world of commerce. More explicit advice along the same lines is found in the saying,* The buyer has need of a hundred eyes, the seller of but one.

Buying and Selling

The bulls make money, the bears make money, but the hogs get slaughtered.

money can be made through buying or selling stock, but greed is fatal; modern saying.

The buyer has need of a hundred eyes, the seller of but one.

stressing the responsibility of a purchaser to examine the goods on offer; English proverb, mid 17th century.

Buy in the cheapest market and sell in the dearest.

sometimes with an implication of sharp practice; English proverb, late 16th century.

Let the buyer beware.

warning that it is up to a buyer to establish the nature and value of a purchase before completing the transaction; English proverb, early 16th century; the saying is also found in the form of the Latin tag *caveat emptor*.

Sell in May and go away (come back on St Leger's Day).

saying related to the cycle of activity on the London Stock Exchange. May, shortly after the start of the financial year, was traditionally a busy time, but during the summer months trading was slack as Londoners (including stockbrokers) took their holiday breaks away from the capital. The full form of the saying refers to the classic

Buying and Selling

St Leger horse race, taken as marking the end of the English summer social calendar.

You buy land, you buy stones; you buy meat, you buy bones.

every purchase has its drawbacks; English proverb, late 17th century.

Cats

See also DOGS

Sayings about cats emphasize not only their independence of humankind, but also their capacity to survive: A cat always lands on its feet.

A cat always lands on its feet.

a cat's natural agility typifies its ability to escape from trouble; traditional saying.

A cat has nine lives.

traditional saying.

A cat may look at a king.

even someone in a lowly position has a right to observe a person of power and influence; English proverb, mid 16th century.

Feed a dog for three days and he will remember your kindness for three years. Feed a cat for three years and she will forget your kindness in three days.

Japanese proverb.

It is better to feed one cat than many mice.

Norwegian proverb.

Touch not the cat but a glove.

but = without, and the cat referred to here is a wild cat; Scottish proverb, early 19th century.

45

Causes and Consequences

Deliberate choice will have a result which may be unwelcome, as in After the feast comes the reckoning. *However, traditional wisdom also emphasizes that something of apparent unimportance may have significant consequences:* The mother of mischief is no bigger than a midge's wing.

After the feast comes the reckoning.

a period of pleasure or indulgence has to be paid for; English proverb, early 17th century, but now chiefly in modern North American use.

As you bake, so shall you brew.

as you begin, so shall you proceed; English proverb, late 16th century.

As you brew, so shall you bake.

your circumstances will be shaped by your own initial actions; English proverb, late 16th century.

As you make your bed, so you must lie upon it.

as you begin, so shall you proceed; English proverb, late 16th century.

As you sow, so you reap.

you will have to endure the consequences of your actions; English proverb, late 15th century; compare **They that sow the wind, shall reap the whirlwind** below.

Causes and Consequences

A fence between makes love more keen.
impediments between lovers are likely to increase fondness;
German proverb.

Good seed makes a bad crop.
something which has a sound basis will do well; English
proverb, mid 16th century.

Great oaks from little acorns grow.
great results may ensue from apparently small beginnings;
English proverb, late 14th century.

He who plants thorns must not expect to gather roses.
Arabic proverb.

If you see a turtle on a fencepost, it didn't get there by accident.
regional American saying.

If you want to see heaven, you have to die yourself.
Indian proverb.

Kill the chicken to scare the monkey.
make an example of those in a weak position to frighten
possible stronger opponents; Chinese saying.

The mother of mischief is no bigger than a midge's wing.
the origin of difficulties can be very small; English proverb,
early 17th century.

Caution

Sow much, reap much; sow little, reap little.
Chinese proverb.

There is reason in the roasting of eggs.
however odd an action may seem, there is a reason for it;
English proverb, mid 17th century.

They that sow the wind, shall reap the whirlwind.
those who have initiated a dangerous course must suffer the
consequences; English proverb, late 16th century; compare
As you sow, so you reap above.

**Who won't be ruled by the rudder must be ruled
by the rock.**
a ship which is not being steered on its course will run on to
a rock; English proverb, mid 17th century.

 Caution

See also DANGER

*We may put ourselves at risk through lack of caution,
but someone who adheres too closely to the advice*
Better be safe than sorry *may miss out on possible
benefits, since* A cat in gloves catches no mice.

Be careful what you wish for, because you may get it.
modern saying, suggesting that the fulfilment of an unwise
objective may turn out to be unwelcome.

Caution

Better be safe than sorry.

urging the wisdom of taking precautions; English proverb, mid 19th century.

A bird in the hand is worth two in the bush.

it is better to accept what one has than to try to get more and risk losing everything; English proverb, mid 15th century.

Call on God, but row away from the rocks.

make an effort to avoid a dangerous situation; Indian proverb.

A cat in gloves catches no mice.

deliberate restraint and caution (or 'pussyfooting') often result in failure to achieve anything; English proverb, late 16th century.

Caution is the parent of safety.

American proverb, early 18th century.

Cross the river by feeling the stones.

Chinese proverb, advising progress through wary experimentation.

Delhi is far away.

warning that unexpected events may intervene in apparently dangerous circumstances; Indian proverb, deriving from the response of the 14th-century Sufi mystic Nizamuddin Aulia to a threat from the Sultan of Delhi

Caution

(the Sultan in fact died before returning home); compare
God is high above, and the tsar is far away and
**The mountains are high, and the emperor is far
away** at GOVERNMENT.

Discretion is the better part of valour.
often used to explain cautious action, and sometimes with
allusion to Shakespeare's *1 Henry IV* (1597), 'The better part
of valour is discretion'; English proverb, late 16th century.

Don't put all your eggs in one basket.
you should not chance everything on a single venture, but
spread the risk; English proverb, mid 17th century.

Don't put up your umbrella before it rains.
do not take defensive action before it becomes necessary;
modern saying.

Duck and cover.
US advice in the event of a missile attack, *c*.1950; associated
particularly with the children's cartoon character 'Bert
the Turtle'.

Full cup, steady hand.
used especially to caution against spoiling a comfortable or
otherwise enviable situation by a careless action; English
proverb, early 11th century.

He who fights and runs away, lives to fight another day.

English proverb, mid 16th century.

He who has been scalded by hot milk, blows even on cold lassi before drinking it.

lassi = an Indian drink, traditionally based on diluted buttermilk or yoghurt, and usually served chilled; Indian proverb; compare **Once bitten by a snake, a man will be afraid of a piece of rope for three years** below.

He who sups with the devil should have a long spoon.

one should be cautious when dealing with dangerous persons; English proverb, late 14th century.

If you can't be good, be careful.

often used as a humorous warning; English proverb, early 20th century; the same idea is found in 11th-century Latin, *si non caste tamen caute*.

Let sleeping dogs lie.

something which may be dangerous or difficult to handle is better left undisturbed; English proverb, late 14th century; compare **Poke a bush, a snake comes out** below.

Let well alone.

often used as a warning against raising problems which will then be difficult to resolve; English proverb, late 16th

Caution

century; compare **Never trouble trouble till trouble troubles you** below.

Look before you leap.
used to advise caution before committing oneself to a course of action; English proverb, mid 14th century.

The more you stir it [a turd] the worse it stinks.
disturbance of something naturally unpleasant will only make it more disagreeable; English proverb, mid 16th century.

Never trouble trouble till trouble troubles you.
another version of the advice that one should let well alone; English proverb, late 19th century.

Once bitten by a snake, a man will be afraid of a piece of rope for three years.
Chinese proverb; compare **He who has been scalded by hot milk, blows even on cold lassi before drinking it** above, and **Once bitten, twice shy** at EXPERIENCE.

Poke a bush, a snake comes out.
warning against unnecessary disturbance; Japanese proverb; compare **Let sleeping dogs lie** above.

Safe bind, safe find.
something kept securely will be readily found again; English proverb, mid 16th century.

Caution

Saw wood and say nothing.

warning against unnecessary disturbance; American proverb, late 19th century.

Second thoughts are best.

it is dangerous to act on one's first impulse without due thought; English proverb, late 16th century.

Steady as she goes!

injunction to hold carefully to the course set; nautical saying.

A stitch in time saves nine.

a small but timely intervention will ensure against the need for much more substantial repair later; English proverb, early 18th century.

Those who play at bowls must look out for rubbers.

one must beware of difficulties associated with a particular activity; *rubber* here is an alteration of *rub*, an obstacle or impediment to the course of a bowl; English proverb, mid 18th century.

Trust, but verify.

Russian proverb, used by President Ronald Reagan during negotiations with the Soviet Union and widely associated with him.

Certainty and Doubt

Trust in Allah, but tie up your camel.
Arab proverb; compare **Put your trust in God, and keep
your powder dry** at PRACTICALITY.

We won't make a drama out of a crisis.
advertising slogan for Commercial Union insurance.

✻ Certainty and Doubt

See also BELIEF, FAITH, INDECISION

*We may be urged to be definite in our views, but
proverbially* Nothing is certain but death and taxes.

**The eyes believe themselves; the ears believe
other people.**
others may persuade us not to believe the evidence of our
own eyes; Greek proverb.

**In matters of principle, stand like a rock; in matters
of taste, swim with the current.**
late 19th-century saying; from the mid 20th century
associated with Thomas Jefferson, in the form 'In matters
of style, swim with the current; in matters of principle,
stand like a rock.'

Nothing is certain but death and taxes.
summarizing what in life is inevitable and inescapable;
English proverb, early 18th century.

Chance and Luck

Against the view that Blind chance sweeps the world along, *there are suggestions that there are ways to make your own fortune:* Diligence is the mother of good luck. *Occasionally, too, the right patronage may be helpful:* The Devil looks after his own.

Accidents will happen (in the best regulated families).

the most orderly arrangements cannot prevent accidents from occurring; English proverb, mid 18th century.

Blind chance sweeps the world along.

American proverb, mid 20th century.

The devil looks after his own.

often used to comment on the good fortune of someone undeserving; English proverb, early 18th century.

The devil's children have the devil's luck.

commenting on the good fortune of someone undeserving; English proverb, late 17th century.

Diligence is the mother of good luck.

success results more from application and practice than from good fortune; English proverb, late 16th century.

Chance and Luck

Fools for luck.
a foolish person is traditionally fortunate; English proverb,
mid 19th century.

**A great fortune depends on luck; a smaller one
on diligence.**
for outstanding success we need good luck as well as the
capacity for hard work; Chinese proverb.

The harder I work, the luckier I get.
modern saying, often as a response to having success
attributed to good fortune.

**If you want to live and thrive, let the spider
run alive.**
It was traditionally unlucky to harm a spider or a spider's
web; English proverb, mid 19th century.

It is better to be born lucky than rich.
often with the implication that riches can be lost or spent,
but that good luck gives one the capacity of improve one's
fortunes; English proverb, mid 17th century.

Lightning never strikes the same place twice.
often used as an encouragement that a particular misfortune
will not be repeated; English proverb, mid 19th century.

Lucky at cards, unlucky in love.
suggesting that good fortune in gambling is balanced by
lack of success in love; English proverb, mid 19th century.

Moses took a chance.

used to urge someone to take a risk; American proverb, mid 20th century.

See a pin and pick it up, all the day you'll have good luck; see a pin and let it lie, bad luck you'll have all day.

extolling the virtues of thrift in small matters; English proverb, mid 19th century.

There is luck in odd numbers.

English proverb, late 16th century.

The third time is the charm.

modern saying; compare **Third time lucky** below.

Third time lucky.

reflecting the idea that three is a lucky number; often used to suggest making another effort after initial failure; English proverb, mid 19th century; compare **The third time is the charm** above.

Throw a lucky man into the sea, and he will come up with a fish in his mouth.

a fortunate person will have further luck; Arabic proverb.

You have two chances, Buckley's and none.

Australian proverb; in Australia, *Buckley's chance* means a slim chance or no chance at all, and is sometimes said to derive from the name of William Buckley (died 1856), who, despite dire predictions as to his chances of survival, lived with the Aboriginals for many years.

 # Change

See also BEGINNING, ENDING

Change may be refreshing (A change is as good as a rest)*, or tiring* (Three removals are as bad as a fire). *However, perhaps more importantly, there is an awareness that some things cannot be changed:* No matter how long a log floats in the river, it will never become a crocodile.

Be sure you can better your condition before you make a change.

American proverb, mid 20th century.

A change is as good as a rest.

suggesting that a change of activity can be refreshing; English proverb, late 19th century.

It is never too late to mend.

one can always try to improve; English proverb, late 16th century.

The leopard does not change his spots.

a person cannot change their essential nature, from the Bible (Jeremiah 13:23), 'Can the Ethiopian change his skin, or the leopard his spots?'; English proverb, mid 16th century; compare **By seeing one spot, you know the entire leopard** at CHARACTER.

Never say never.

used as a warning against over-confidence that circumstances cannot change; late 20th century saying; compare **Never is a long time** and TIME.

New brooms sweep clean.

often used in the context of someone newly appointed to a post who is making changes in personnel and procedures; English proverb, mid 16th century.

New lords, new laws.

new authorities are likely to change existing rules; English proverb, mid 16th century.

No matter how long a log floats in the river, it will never become a crocodile.

essential characteristics will not change; African proverb; compare **Feeding a snake with milk will not change its poisonous nature** at CHARACTER.

No more Mr Nice Guy.

said to assert that one will no longer be amiable or cooperative; mid 20th-century saying.

Nothing is for ever.

late 20th-century saying.

Change

Other times, other manners.
used in resignation or consolation; English proverb, late
16th century.

Out with the old, in with the new.
modern saying.

Semper eadem.
Latin, meaning 'Ever the same', the motto of Elizabeth I
(1533–1603).

There are no birds in last year's nest.
circumstances have changed, and former opportunities are
no longer there; English proverb, early 17th century.

Three removals are as bad as a fire.
moving house is so disruptive and unsettling, that the
effects of doing it three times are as devastating as a house
fire; English proverb, mid 18th century.

Times change and we with time.
we adapt in response to changes in the world around us;
English proverb, late 16th century.

**To change, and change for the better, are two
different things.**
German proverb.

Variety is the spice of life.

English proverb, late 18th century, originally with allusion
to William Cowper's *The Task* (1785), 'Variety's the very
spice of life,/That gives it all its flavour.'

When the music changes, so does the dance.

a reminder that we need to change with the times;
African proverb.

**When the wind of change blows, some build walls,
others build windmills.**

modern saying, sometimes claimed to be an old Chinese
proverb, but found only from the late 20th century.

You can't put new wine in old bottles.

often used in relation to the introduction of new ideas or
practices; English proverb, early 20th century, from the
Bible (Matthew 9:17), 'Neither do men put new wine into
old bottles: else the bottles break, and the wine runneth out,
and the bottles perish.'

Character

See also THE HUMAN RACE, REPUTATION

*A number of sayings reflect on essential characteristics
displayed through outward appearance:* By seeing one
spot, you know the entire leopard. *However, there is
some warning against making too ready assumptions*

Character

from outer circumstances: The man who is born in a stable is not a horse.

An ape's an ape, a varlet's a varlet, though they be clad in silk or scarlet.
inward nature cannot be overcome by outward show; English proverb, mid 16th century.

A bad penny always turns up.
referring to the inevitable return of an unwanted or disreputable person; English proverb, mid 18th century.

The bee sucks honey where the spider sucks poison.
we make the best or worst of things depending on our own nature; English proverb.

Better a good cow than a cow of a good kind.
good character is more important than distinguished lineage; English proverb, early 20th century.

By seeing one spot, you know the entire leopard.
Japanese proverb; compare **The leopard does not change his spots** at CHANGE.

Cet animal est très méchant: Quand on l'attaque, il se défend **['This animal is very vicious: when attacked, it defends itself'].**
ironic recognition that a natural urge to defend yourself may be interpreted as aggression; French proverb.

Character is what we are; reputation is what others think we are.

American proverb, mid 20th century.

The child is the father of the man.

asserting the unity of character from childhood to adult life; English proverb, early 19th century; from Wordsworth's lines 'The Child is father of the Man; And I could wish my days to be Bound each to each by natural piety.'

Eagles don't catch flies.

great or important persons do not concern themselves with trifling matters; English proverb, mid 16th century.

Feeding a snake with milk will not change its poisonous nature.

kindness will not alter a bad character; Indian proverb; compare **No matter how long a log floats in the river, it will never become a crocodile** at CHANGE.

Iron sharpens iron.

friends of the same calibre can strengthen one another; modern saying, with biblical allusion to Proverbs 27:17, 'Iron sharpeneth iron; so a man sharpeneth the countenance of his friend.'

It takes all sorts to make a world.

often used in recognition that a particular group may encompass a wide range of character and background; English proverb, early 17th century.

Character

Like a fence, character cannot be strengthened by whitewash.
American proverb, mid 20th century.

The man who is born in a stable is not a horse.
sometimes attributed to the Duke of Wellington, who asserted that being born in Ireland did not make him Irish; English proverb, mid 19th century.

Once a —, always a —.
a particular way of life produces traits that cannot be eradicated; English proverb, early 17th century; compare **Once a priest, always a priest** at CLERGY.

The same fire that hardens the egg melts the butter.
different people will react in different ways to the same experiences; modern saying, but the idea is found in the early 17th century in the words of Francis Bacon (1561–1623), 'In one and the same fire, clay grows hard and wax melts.'

A sleeping fox counts hens in his dreams.
particular characteristics affect all we do; Russian proverb.

Still waters run deep.
now commonly used to assert that a placid exterior hides a passionate nature; English proverb, early 15th century; compare **Where the river is deepest, it makes the least noise** below.

A stream cannot rise above its source.

used to suggest that a person's natural level is set by their ultimate origin; English proverb, mid 17th century.

The style is the man.

one's chosen style reflects one's essential characteristics; English proverb, early 20th century, although a similar thought is found earlier in French, in the Comte de Buffon's words to the Académie Française on 25 August 1753, 'These things [subject matter] are external to the man; style is the man.'

There's many a good cock come out of a tattered bag.

something good may emerge from unpromising surroundings (the reference is to cockfighting); English proverb, late 19th century.

The tree is known by its fruit.

a person is judged by what they do and produce; English proverb, early 16th century.

What can you expect from a pig but a grunt?

used rhetorically of coarse or boorish behaviour; English proverb, mid 18th century.

What's bred in the bone will come out in the flesh.

inherent characteristics will in the end become apparent; English proverb, late 15th century.

Charity

When the going gets tough, the tough get going.
pressure acts as a stimulus to the strong; English
proverb, mid 20th century, often used by Joseph Kennedy
(1888–1969) as an injunction to his children.

Where the river is deepest, it makes the least noise.
Italian proverb; compare **Still waters run deep** above.

**You cannot dream yourself into a character, you
must forge one out for yourself.**
American proverb, mid 20th century.

 # Charity

See also GENEROSITY

Together with praise for the natural springs of charity,
The roots of charity are always green, *there may be
a note of self-interest:* Keep your own fish-guts for
your own sea-maws.

Charity begins at home.
you should look first to needs in your immediate vicinity;
English proverb, late 14th century.

**Charity is not a bone you throw to a dog but a bone
you share with a dog.**
the recipient of one's charity should not be treated as an
inferior; American proverb, mid 20th century.

Charity sees the need, not the cause.

true charity succours need regardless of whether the
needy person is responsible for their own situation;
German proverb.

**Give a man a fish, and you feed him for a day;
show him how to catch fish, and you feed him
for a lifetime.**

mid 20th century saying, perhaps deriving from a Chinese
saying; compare **Who teaches me for a day, is my father
for a lifetime** at TEACHING.

**If everyone gives a thread, the poor man will
have a shirt.**

a little from each person makes an effective whole;
Russian proverb.

Keep your own fish-guts for your own sea-maws.

any surplus product should be offered first to those in need
who are closest to you; Scottish proverb, early 18th century.

The roots of charity are always green.

true generosity constantly renews itself; American proverb,
mid 20th century.

Service is the rent we pay for our room on earth.

modern saying, deriving from the admission ceremony of
Toc H, a society, originally of ex-servicemen and women,
founded by Tubby Clayton (1885–1972) after the First

World War to promote Christian fellowship and
social service.

 Children

See also THE FAMILY, PARENTS, YOUTH

*Changes in attitude have moved the focus on
child-rearing from the repressive* Children should be
seen and not heard *and* Spare the rod, and spoil the
child *to the duty of society to nurture as expressed by
the African saying,* It takes a village to raise a child.

**And the child that is born on the Sabbath day,
Is bonny, and blithe, and good and gay.**
line from a traditional rhyme (compare qualities associated
with birth on other days at entries under BEAUTY, GIFTS,
SORROW, TRAVEL, and WORK).

**The art of being a parent consists of sleeping when
the baby isn't looking.**
American proverb, mid 20th century.

Children: one is one, two is fun, three is a houseful.
American proverb, mid 20th century.

Children should be seen and not heard.
originally applied specifically to (young) women; English
proverb, early 15th century.

It takes a village to raise a child.

many in the community have a role in a child's development; African proverb (Yoruba).

Little children, little sorrows; big children, great sorrows.

even when grown up, children are likely to be a source of concern to their parents; Danish proverb.

No moon, no man.

recording the traditional belief that a child born at the time of the new moon or just before its appearance will not live to grow up; English proverb, late 19th century.

Spare the rod and spoil the child.

the result of not disciplining a child is to spoil it; English proverb, early 11th century, sometimes with allusion to the Bible (Proverbs 13:24), 'He that spareth his rod hateth his son.'

Choice

See also INDECISION

Choice may be inevitable, as in A door must be either shut or open, *but it is noticeable how often the view is that we find ourselves choosing between unpalatable options:* Small choice in rotten apples.

Choice

Better red than dead.

slogan of nuclear disarmament campaigners, late 1950s.

Different strokes for different folks.

different ways of doing something are appropriate for
different people (the saying is of US origin, and *strokes*
here means 'comforting gestures of approval'); late
20th-century saying.

A door must be either shut or open.

said of two mutually exclusive alternatives; English proverb,
mid 18th century.

He that has a choice has trouble.

choosing between two things or persons may cause
difficulties; American proverb, mid 20th century.

No man can serve two masters.

English proverb, early 14th century.

The obvious choice is usually a quick regret.

selection on outward appearance alone soon disappoints;
American proverb, mid 20th century.

Of two evils choose the less.

English proverb, late 14th century.

Small choice in rotten apples.

if all options are unpalatable there is little choice to be had;
English proverb, late 16th century.

**They offered death so you would be happy
with a fever.**

a worse possibility makes something inherently unwelcome
acceptable; Persian proverb.

You pays your money and you takes your choice.

said when there is little or nothing to choose between two
options; English proverb, mid 19th century.

The Christian Church

See also CLERGY, GOD, RELIGION

*The essential strength of the Church is seen in its
capacity to withstand persecution:* The church is an
anvil which has worn out many hammers.

The blood of the martyrs is the seed of the Church.

persecution causes the Church to grow; English proverb,
mid 16th century, perhaps ultimately deriving from
the *Apologeticus* of the Roman theologian Tertullian
(*c.* AD 160–*c.*225), 'As often as we are mown down by you,
the more we grow in numbers; the blood of Christians
is the seed.

The Christian Church

Christ has no body now on earth but yours, no hands but yours, no feet but yours, yours are the eyes through which he looks compassion on this world, yours are the feet with which he is to go about doing good.

modern saying, often attributed to St Teresa of Ávila (1512–82), but not found in her writings.

The Christians to the lions!

saying reported by the Roman theologian Tertullian (c. AD 160–c.225) in his *Apologeticus*, 'If the Tiber rises, if the Nile does not rise, if the heavens give no rain, if there is an earthquake, famine, or pestilence, straightway the cry is…'

The church is an anvil which has worn out many hammers.

the passive strength of Christianity will outlast aggression; English proverb, mid 19th century.

A church is God between four walls.

American proverb, mid 20th century.

Meat and mass never hindered man.

indicating human need for physical and spiritual sustenance; English proverb, early 17th century.

The nearer the church, the farther from God.

sometimes used to indicate a lack of true spirituality where it is most likely to be found; English proverb, early 14th century.

You can't build a church with stumbling-blocks.

members of a church need to work together in fellowship;
American proverb, mid 20th century.

Christmas

*Sayings about Christmas give particular emphasis to
preparations for celebration, from the gifts appropriate
to the Twelve Days to the anticipated feasting:*
Christmas is coming, and the goose is getting fat.

**Christmas comes but once a year, and when it
comes it brings good cheer.**

traditional saying, going back to the 16th century.

Christmas is coming, and the goose is getting fat.

from a traditional rhyme, recorded from the 19th century
(goose was traditional Christmas fare).

**Christmas with the family, Easter with whomever
you want.**

Italian proverb, *Natale con i tuoi, Pasqua con chi vuoi.*

A green Yule makes a fat churchyard.

a mild winter is traditionally unhealthy (*Yule* is an archaic
term for Christmas); English proverb, mid 17th century.

Only — shopping days to Christmas.
the imminence of Christmas expressed in commercial terms.

Circumstance and Situation

See also CHANGE

It is as well to come to terms with circumstances, a consensus expressed in the advice offered by the Indian proverb, If you live in the river, you should make friends with the crocodile.

Although the branch is broken off, the trunk remains.
damage, while unpleasant, is not necessarily disastrous; Maori saying.

Circumstances alter cases.
a general principle may be modified in the light of particular circumstances; English proverb, late 17th century.

If you do not know where you have been, you cannot know where you are going.
understanding of your own situation is essential for effective action; African proverb.

Circumstance and Situation

If you live in the river, you should make friends with the crocodile.

Indian proverb.

May you live in interesting times.

used ironically, as eventful times are often dangerous or unpleasant; modern saying, said to derive from a Chinese curse, but likely to be apocryphal.

New circumstances, new controls.

American proverb, mid 20th century.

No rose without a thorn.

even the pleasantest circumstances have their drawbacks; English proverb, mid 15th century.

One day honey, one day onions.

Arab proverb.

One man's loss is another man's gain.

often said by the gainer in self-congratulation; English proverb, early 16th century.

A rolling stone gathers no moss.

used to imply that someone who does not settle down will not prosper, or form lasting ties; English proverb, mid 14th century.

Cities

There's a time and place for everything.
often used as a warning against doing or saying something at a particular time or in a particular situation; English proverb, early 16th century.

There's no great loss without some gain.
said in consolation or resignation; English proverb, mid 17th century.

The wheel has come full circle.
the situation has returned to what it was in the past, as if completing a cycle, with reference to Shakespeare's *King Lear* 'The wheel is come full circle.'

 # Cities

See TOWNS AND CITIES

 # Clergy

See also THE CHRISTIAN CHURCH

Sayings relating to the clerical profession include the rather bleak assessment of the likely pressure on a cleric's family: Clergyman's sons always turn out badly. *However, there is no going back:* Once a priest, always a priest.

Clergymen's sons always turn out badly.

the implication is that the weight of expectation on clergymen's children is often itself damaging; English proverb, late 19th century.

Like people, like priest.

English proverb, late 16th century; from the Bible (Hosea 4:9), 'And there shall be like people, like priest.'

Nobody is born learned; bishops are made of men.

American proverb, mid 20th century.

Once a priest, always a priest.

English proverb, mid 19th century; compare **Once a —, always a —** at CHARACTER.

Computing

See also TECHNOLOGY

Sayings about the world of computing date from early days of the technology, when the instruction Do not fold, spindle or mutilate *was an important warning. However, some sayings are timeless:* Garbage in, garbage out *remains true through all developments.*

Do not fold, spindle or mutilate.

instruction on punched cards (1950s, and in differing forms from the 1930s).

Computing

Garbage in, garbage out.
in computing, incorrect or faulty input will always cause poor output; mid 20th century saying.

If you can't do it in Fortran, do it in assembly language. If you can't do it in assembly language, it's not worth doing.
saying on computer programming (*Fortran* = a high-level programming language used especially for scientific calculations).

It's not a bug, it's a feature.
bug = an error in a computer program or system; late 20th-century saying.

No manager ever got fired for buying IBM.
IBM advertising slogan.

There is no patch for stupid.
21st-century saying relating to cybersecurity, implying that the human element is the weakest part of any system.

To err is human but to really foul things up requires a computer.
late 20th-century saying; compare **to err is human (to forgive divine)** at MISTAKES.

Conscience

See also FORGIVENESS

Proverbial wisdom tends to dwell on the uncomfortable effects of a bad conscience. While A clean conscience is a good pillow, *permitting easy sleep, awareness of guilt makes the waking life unpleasant:* Evil doers are evil dreaders.

A clean conscience is a good pillow.

a clear conscience enables its possessor to sleep soundly; English proverb, early 18th century.

Conscience gets a lot of credit that belongs to cold feet.

American proverb, mid 20th century.

Do right and fear no man.

English proverb, mid 15th century.

Evil doers are evil dreaders.

someone engaged in wrongdoing is likely to be nervous and suspicious of others; English proverb, mid 16th century.

A guilty conscience needs no accuser.

awareness of one's own guilt has the same effect as an accusation; English proverb, late 14th century.

Let your conscience be your guide.

American proverb, mid 20th century.

Consequences

A quiet conscience sleeps in thunder.

someone with an untroubled conscience will sleep
undisturbed whatever the noise; English proverb, late
16th century.

 # Consequences

See CAUSES AND CONSEQUENCES

 # Cooking

See also EATING, FOOD

Good equipment is important (A cook is no better
than her stove)*, but you cannot always judge by
outward appearances:* All are not cooks who sport
white caps and carry long knives.

**All are not cooks who sport white caps and carry
long knives.**

American proverb, mid 20th century.

A cook is no better than her stove.

American proverb, mid 20th century.

**Fish, to taste good, must swim three times—in
water, in butter, and in wine.**

the best way to cook fish; Polish proverb.

God sends meat, but the Devil sends cooks.
anything which is in itself good or useful may be spoiled or perverted by the use to which it is put; English proverb, mid 16th century.

It is a poor cook that cannot lick his own fingers.
a good cook assesses their food with their own sense of taste; English proverb.

Keep one eye on the frying-pan, and one on the cat.
Italian proverb.

Cooperation

Sayings about cooperation emphasize the positive side of working with others, as in When spider webs unite, they can tie up a lion. *However, the dangers of not cooperating are also considered:* If you don't believe in cooperation, watch what happens to a wagon when one wheel comes off.

All arts are brothers; each is a light to the other.
American proverb, mid 19th century.

A chain is no stronger than its weakest link.
often used when identifying a particular point of vulnerability; English proverb, mid 19th century; compare **You are the weakest link . . . goodbye** at STRENGTH AND WEAKNESS.

Cooperation

Cross the river in a crowd, and the crocodile won't eat you.
Madagascar saying.

Dog does not eat dog.
people of the same profession should not attack each other;
English proverb, mid 16th century.

Each of us at a handle of the basket.
Maori proverb.

Every little helps.
English proverb, early 17th century.

Four eyes see more than two.
two people are more observant than one alone; English
proverb, late 16th century.

Hawks will not pick out hawks' eyes.
powerful people from the same group will not attack one
another; English proverb, late 16th century.

**He who travels fast, travels alone, and he who
travels far, travels in the company of others.**
African proverb.

**If you don't believe in cooperation, watch what
happens to a wagon when one wheel comes off.**
American proverb, mid 20th century.

If you think cooperation is unnecessary, just try running your car a while on three wheels.

American proverb, mid 20th century.

It takes two to make a bargain.

often used to imply that both parties must be prepared to give some ground; English proverb, late 16th century.

It takes two to tango.

meaning that a cooperative venture requires a contribution from both participants; mid 20th-century saying, from the 1952 song by Al Hoffman and Dick Manning.

Little birds that can sing and won't sing must be made to sing.

those who refuse to obey or cooperate will be forced to do so; English proverb, late 17th century.

Many hands make light work.

often used as an encouragement to join in with assistance; English proverb, mid 14th century.

One good turn deserves another.

English proverb, early 15th century.

One hand washes the other.

referring to cooperation between two closely linked persons or organizations; English proverb, late 16th century.

Cooperation

A single arrow is easily broken, but not ten in a bundle.
when people combine, they can resist attack;
Japanese proverb.

A single bracelet does not jingle.
to make an effect we need the help of others; African proverb.

There is honour among thieves.
sometimes used ironically; English proverb, early
19th century.

A trouble shared is a trouble halved.
discussing a problem will lessen its impact; English proverb,
mid 20th century.

Union is strength.
English proverb, mid 17th century; *unity* is a popular
alternative for *union*, especially when used as a
trade-union slogan.

United we stand, divided we fall.
a watchword of the American Revolution, English proverb,
late 18th century.

We live in each other's shadow.
Irish proverb.

When spider webs unite, they can tie up a lion.
African proverb.

When the lips are gone, the teeth are cold.
Chinese proverb.

With your food basket, and with my food basket, the guest will have enough.
Maori proverb.

Corruption

Sayings such as A golden key can open any door *remind us that there is always likely to be someone who is open to bribery—and that the practice may spread, given that* The rotten apple injures its neighbour.

Corruption will find a dozen alibis for its evil deeds.
American proverb, mid 20th century.

Every man has his price.
everyone is susceptible to the right bribe; English proverb, mid 18th century.

A golden key can open any door.
any access is guaranteed if enough money is offered; English proverb, late 16th century.

If gold rusts, what will iron do?
if someone of admirable character succumbs to temptation, what is likely to happen to a person of less upright character; English proverb.

Countries and Peoples

It's not what you know, it's who you know.

stressing the importance of personal influence; late 20th century saying.

The rotten apple injures its neighbour.

often used to mean that one corrupt person in an organization is likely to affect others; English proverb, mid 14th century.

When money speaks, the truth keeps silent.

Russian proverb.

✿ Countries and Peoples

Sayings about countries and peoples may reflect either a cherished self-image (An Englishman's word is his bond), *or a less flattering opinion from someone who does not belong to the people concerned:* Scratch a Russian and you find a Tartar.

Advance Australia.

catchphrase used as a patriotic slogan or motto, mid 19th century onwards; the national anthem of Australia (officially adopted in 1984) includes the lines, 'In joyful strains then let us sing Advance Australia fair.'

A mare usque ad mare.

Latin, meaning 'From sea unto sea'; motto of Canada, taken from the Bible (Psalm 72), 'He shall have dominion also from sea to sea, and from the river unto the ends of the earth.'

America is a tune. It must be sung together.
American proverb, mid 20th century.

Australians wouldn't give a XXXX for anything else.
advertising slogan for Castlemaine lager, 1986 onwards.

England is the paradise of women, the hell of horses, and the purgatory of servants.
English proverb, late 16th century.

England's difficulty is Ireland's opportunity.
associated with the aspirations of Irish nationalism; English proverb, mid 19th century.

An Englishman's word is his bond.
a promise given is regarded as having the force of a legal agreement; English proverb, early 16th century.

Every land has its own law.
Scottish proverb, early 17th century, used to emphasize the individuality of a nation or group.

Every Turk is born a soldier.
Turkish saying.

God made the world, but the Dutch made Holland.
traditional saying, recorded from the 19th century.

Good Americans when they die go to Paris.
coinage attributed to Thomas Gold Appleton (1812–84);
American proverb, mid 19th century.

It is a striking coincidence that the word American ends in *can*.
American proverb, mid 20th century.

A nation without a language is a nation without a heart.
Welsh proverb.

Scratch a Russian and you find a Tartar.
if a person is harmed their real national character will be
revealed; English proverb, early 19th century.

✽ The Country and the Town

The contrast between urban and rural life embodies what is often seen as a key cultural division.

An everyday story of country folk.
traditional summary of the BBC's long-running radio soap
opera *The Archers*.

God made the country and man made the town.
contrasting rural and urban life; English proverb, mid
17th century, in this form from William Cowper's poem
The Task (1785).

If you have not lived in the country, you do not know what hardship means.

contrasting rural and urban poverty; Chinese proverb.

You can take the boy out of the country but you can't take the country out of the boy.

even when a person moves away from the place they were brought up in, they retain its essential manners and customs; English proverb, mid 20th century.

Courage

See also DANGER, FEAR

Courage may be admirable itself, but proverbial wisdom also stresses the practical advantages that it may bring: Fortune favours the brave.

Attack is the best form of defence.

English proverb, late 18th century; compare **The best defence is a good offence** below.

The best defence is a good offence.

late 20th-century American version of **Attack is the best form of defence** above.

A bully is always a coward.

English proverb, early 19th century.

Courage

Courage is fear that has said its prayers.

American proverb, mid 20th century.

Courage without conduct is like a ship without ballast.

American proverb, mid 20th century.

Don't cry before you're hurt.

sometimes used as a warning against appealing for sympathy on the assumption of an unpleasant outcome; English proverb, mid 16th century.

Faint heart never won fair lady.

often used as an encouragement to action; English proverb, mid 16th century.

For every Pharaoh there is a Moses.

a liberator will arise against every oppressor; Middle Eastern proverb.

Fortune favours the brave.

a person who acts bravely is likely to be successful; English proverb, late 14th century, originally often with allusion to *Phormio* by the Roman comic dramatist Terence, 'Fortune assists the brave', and Virgil *The Aeneid*, 'Fortune assists the bold.'

None but the brave deserve the fair.

English proverb, late 17th century, from Dryden's poem *Alexander's Feast* (1697), 'None but the brave deserves the fair.'

You never know what you can do till you try.

often used as encouragement to the reluctant; English proverb, early 19th century.

Crime and Punishment

See also GUILT, JUSTICE, THE LAW, MURDER

From Ill gotten goods never thrive *in the 16th century, to* Crime doesn't pay *in the 20th century, there is a consensus that wrongdoing is unlikely benefit the perpetrator—even if society does not follow the kind of draconian practice enshrined in the recommendation,* Hang a thief when he's young, and he'll no steal when he's old.

A conservative is a liberal who's been mugged.

American saying, 1980s.

Crime doesn't pay.

American proverb, early 20th century; a slogan of the FBI and the cartoon detective Dick Tracy.

Crime leaves a trail like a water beetle.

Malay proverb.

Crime must be concealed by crime.

American proverb, mid 20th century.

Crime and Punishment

Hang a thief when he's young, and he'll no steal when he's old.

Scottish proverbial saying, early 19th century.

If there were no receivers, there would be no thieves.

English proverb, late 14th century.

Ill gotten goods never thrive.

something which is acquired dishonestly is unlikely to be the basis of lasting prosperity; English proverb, early 16th century.

Little thieves are hanged, but great ones escape.

sufficient power and influence can ensure that a wrongdoer is not punished; English proverb, mid 17th century.

Opportunity makes a thief.

often used to imply that the carelessness of the person who is robbed has contributed to the crime; English proverb, early 13th century.

Three strikes and you're out.

referring to legislation which provides that an offender's third felony is punishable by life imprisonment or other severe sentence; deriving from the terminology of baseball, in which a batter who has had three strikes, or three fair opportunities of hitting the ball, is out; late 20th-century saying.

When thieves fall out, honest men come by their own.

meaning that it is through thieves quarrelling over their stolen goods that they are likely to be caught, and the goods recovered; English proverb, mid 16th century.

You'll die facing the monument.

warning of the end of a life of crime; in Glasgow, prisoners were hanged facing Nelson's Monument on Glasgow Green; Scottish proverb.

Crises

Sayings on this topic focus on how to meet a crisis, whether by 'keeping calm' or taking more active measures.

Any port in a storm.

when one is in trouble or difficulty, support or shelter from any source is welcome; English proverb, mid 18th century.

Keep calm and carry on.

poster designed by the Ministry of Information in 1939 but not used in the Second World War; rediscovered and popularized in the early 21st century.

Never waste a good crisis.
modern saying in various forms, often linked with the advice 'Never let a serious crisis go to waste' of Rahm Emmanuel, Chief of Staff in Barack Obama's first administration.

When disaster strikes and all hope is gone, get down on your knees and pray for Shackleton.
paraphrase of Apsley Cherry-Garrard's tribute to the Antarctic explorer Ernest Shackleton (1874–1922) by British geologist Raymond Priestley (1886–1974) in a lecture 'Twentieth Century Man against Antarctica' (1950).

Criticism

See also LIKES AND DISLIKES

While self-examination can be a wholesome discipline, we should not be too ready to criticize others:
Don't judge a man till you've walked two moons in his moccasins.

The best place for criticism is in front of your mirror.
judge yourself before others; American proverb, mid 20th century.

Criticism is something you can avoid by saying nothing, doing nothing, and being nothing.

abstaining from criticism will result in complete inaction; American proverb, mid 20th century.

Don't judge a man till you've walked two moons in his moccasins.

warning against judging without understanding circumstances; modern saying, said to be of Native American origin.

Custom and Habit ❀

Sayings about custom tend towards the negative: there is a perception that enshrined practice is likely to lead to someone being less able to deal with changes: You can't teach an old dog new tricks.

A bad custom is like a good cake, better broken than kept.

we should use our judgement to decide whether a custom is worthy of respect; English proverb.

Custom is mummified by habit and glorified by law.

American proverb, mid 20th century.

Habits are cobwebs at first, and cables at last.

traditional saying, recorded from the 19th century.

Custom and Habit

Old habits die hard.
it is difficult to break long-established habits; English proverb, mid 18th century.

Sow an act, and reap a habit.
recommending the development of good practice; English proverb.

What is new cannot be true.
used to imply that innovation is less soundly based than custom which has been proved by experience; English proverb, mid 17th century.

You cannot shift an old tree without it dying.
often used to suggest the risk involved in moving an elderly person who has lived in the same place for many years; English proverb, early 16th century.

You can't teach an old dog new tricks.
someone who is already set in their ways is not able to learn new ways of doing things; English proverb, mid 16th century.

Dance

Dancing may require some innate ability—You need more than dancing shoes to be a dancer—*but dancing is still seen as a natural form of expression:* We're fools whether we dance or not, so we might as well dance.

One who cannot dance blames the uneven floor.

Indian proverb; compare **A bad workman blames his tools** at APOLOGY AND EXCUSES.

We're fools whether we dance or not, so we might as well dance.

modern saying, claimed to be a Japanese proverb.

When you go to dance, take heed whom you take by the hand.

English proverb, early 17th century.

You need more than dancing shoes to be a dancer.

American proverb, mid 20th century.

Danger

See also CAUTION, COURAGE, FEAR

A risk may be taken rightly, since The post of honour is the post of danger, *but peril can result from overconfidence:* When the lion shows its teeth, don't assume that it is smiling.

Danger

Adventures are to the adventurous.
the person who wants exciting things to happen must take the initiative; English proverb, mid 19th century.

A common danger causes common action.
American proverb, mid 20th century.

Heaven protects children, sailors, and drunken men.
often used (in a number of variant forms) to imply that someone unable to look after themselves has been undeservedly lucky; English proverb, mid 19th century.

He who rides a tiger is afraid to dismount.
once a dangerous or troublesome venture is begun, the safest course is to carry it through to the end; English proverb, late 19th century.

If you play with fire you get burnt.
if you involve yourself with something potentially dangerous you are likely to be hurt; English proverb, late 19th century.

It is the calm and silent water that drowns the man.
the greatest danger may be concealed beneath an innocent appearance; African proverb.

Just when you thought it was safe to go back in the water.
advertising copy for the film *Jaws 2* (1978), featuring the return of the great white shark to bathing beaches.

Light the blue touch paper and retire immediately.

traditional instruction for lighting fireworks.

More than one yew bow in Chester.

you may escape danger once, but not a second time (*Chester* representing the English, the traditional enemy for Wales); Welsh proverb.

The post of honour is the post of danger.

English proverb, mid 16th century.

Three things are not to be trusted; a cow's horn, a dog's tooth, and a horse's hoof.

one may be gored, bitten, or kicked, without warning; English proverb, late 14th century.

We have no friends but the mountains.

inhospitable terrain is more reliable than an ally as a source of safety; Kurdish proverb.

When the lion shows its teeth, don't assume that it is smiling.

a warning sign from a source of power should not be taken lightly; Arab proverb.

When you ask a bear to dance, you can't stop just because you are tired.

modern American saying.

Death

Who dares wins.

motto of the British Special Air Service regiment;
from 1942.

The wolves are well fed and the sheep are safe.

when a predator's immediate needs have been satisfied,
there is temporary safety for the prey; Russian proverb.

Women and children first.

order given on a ship in difficulty, indicating that women
and children should be allowed onto the lifeboats before
men; in allusive (and often humorous) use, warning of a
risky or unpleasant situation; from the mid 19th century.

❀ Death

See also MOURNING

*The end of life may offer an escape from some pressures,
since* Death pays all debts, *but the main note is one
of resignation in the face of the inevitable:* There is a
remedy for everything except death.

As a tree falls, so shall it lie.

one should not alter one's long-established practices and
customs because of approaching death; English proverb,
mid 16th century, from the Bible (Ecclesiastes 11:3), 'In the
place where the tree falleth, there it shall be.'

Blessed are the dead that the rain rains on.

English proverb, early 17th century.

[Death is] Nature's way of telling you to slow down.

American life insurance saying, in *Newsweek* 25 April 1960.

Death is the great leveller.

all people will be equal in death, whatever their material prosperity; English proverb, early 18th century.

Death pays all debts.

the death of a person cancels out their obligations; English proverb, early 17th century.

Et in Arcadia ego.

Latin tomb inscription, 'And I too in Arcadia', of disputed meaning, often depicted in classical paintings, notably by Poussin in 1655.

One funeral makes many.

sometimes with the implication that attendance at a deathbed or funeral may have fatal consequences; English proverb, late 19th century.

Stone-dead hath no fellow.

traditionally used by advocates of the death penalty, to suggest that only when a dangerous person is dead can one be sure that they will pose no further threat; English proverb, mid 17th century.

Debt and Borrowing

There is a remedy for everything except death.
English proverb, mid 15th century.

You can only die once.
used to encourage someone in a dangerous or difficult
enterprise; English proverb, mid 15th century.

Young men may die, but old men must die.
death is inevitable for all, and can at best be postponed until
old age; English proverb, mid 16th century.

✻ Debt and Borrowing

See also THRIFT

*The idea that a national debt could be a national
blessing might sound upbeat, but more sayings stress the
dangers of getting into debt, summed up generally in
the 15th-century assertion* He that goes a-borrowing,
goes a-sorrowing.

Better to go to bed supperless than rise in debt.
English proverb, mid 17th-century saying.

A borrowed cloak does not keep you warm.
Arabic proverb, warning against relying on resources
borrowed from another.

Debt and Borrowing

Have a horse of your own, and you may borrow another's.

evidence that you have resources of your own makes it more likely that you will be lent something; English proverb.

He that goes a-borrowing, goes a-sorrowing.

involving oneself in debt is likely to lead to unhappiness; English proverb, late 15th century.

Lend your money and lose your friend.

debt puts a strain on friendship; English proverb, late 15th century.

A man in debt is caught in a net.

American proverb, mid 20th century.

A national debt, if it is not excessive, will be to us a national blessing.

American proverb; often attributed to the American politician Alexander Hamilton (*c*.1755–1804).

Neither a borrower, nor a lender be.

advising caution in financial dealings with others; English proverb, early 17th century, from the words of Polonius to his son Laertes in Shakespeare *Hamlet* (1601), 'Neither a borrower, nor a lender be, For loan oft loses both itself and friend.'

Deception

Out of debt, out of danger.

someone in debt is vulnerable and at risk from others;
English proverb, mid 17th century.

Short reckonings make long friends.

the prompt settlement of any debt between friends ensures
that their friendship will not be damaged; English proverb,
mid 16th century.

 # Deception

See also LIES

*Deception may not benefit the perpetrator, since we are
told that* Cheats never prosper, *but there is also a
warning that we have some responsibility for ensuring
that we are not deceived:* Fool me once, shame on you;
fool me twice, shame on me.

Cheats never prosper.

English proverb, early 19th century.

Deceit is a lie, that wears a smile.

American proverb, mid 20th century.

Fool me once, shame on you; fool me twice, shame on me.

if someone is deceived twice by the same person, their own
stupidity is to blame; late 20th-century saying.

The quickness of the hand deceives the eye.
saying associated with the art of conjuring; recorded from
the mid 19th century.

Deeds

See WORDS AND DEEDS

Defiance

See also DETERMINATION

Apart from the traditional reflection that You can take
a horse to water, but you can't make him drink,
*defiance is often expressed through a slogan, from the
17th-century* No surrender! *to the anti-Poll Tax cry*
Can't pay, won't pay *of the early 1990s.*

Burn, baby, burn.
black extremist slogan in use during the Los Angeles riots,
August 1965.

Can't pay, won't pay.
anti-Poll Tax slogan, *c.*1990.

Ils ne passeront pas.
French, 'They shall not pass', slogan used by the French
army at the defence of Verdun in 1916; variously attributed
to Marshal Pétain and to General Robert Nivelle, and

Defiance

subsequently taken up by Republicans in the Spanish Civil War in the form *No pasarán!*

Nemo me impune lacessit.

Latin, 'No one provokes me with impunity', motto of the Crown of Scotland and of all Scottish regiments.

No surrender!

Protestant Northern Irish slogan originating with the defenders of Derry against the Catholic forces of James II in 1689.

They haif said: Quhat say they? Lat thame say.

motto of the Earl Marischal of Scotland, inscribed at Marischal College, Aberdeen, 1593; a similarly defiant motto in Greek has been found engraved in remains from classical antiquity.

You can take a horse to the water, but you can't make him drink.

even if you create the right circumstances you cannot persuade someone to do something against their will; English proverb, late 12th century.

The wiser man gives in.

obstinate defiance is likely to be damaging to yourself; German proverb.

Delay

See HASTE AND DELAY

Determination

See also DEFIANCE

Refusal to be deterred by apparent failure can overcome both disappointment, as in the encouraging Fall seven times, stand up eight, *and difficult circumstances, since* A determined fellow can do more with a rusty monkey wrench than a lot of people can with a machine shop.

The best fish swim near the bottom.
patience and persistence are necessary for the best results; English proverb.

Beyond mountains there are more mountains.
overcoming the first obstacle is likely to bring you face to face with another; Haitian proverb.

Constant dropping wears away a stone.
primarily used to mean that persistence will achieve a difficult or unlikely object; English proverb, mid 13th century.

Determination

A determined fellow can do more with a rusty monkey wrench than a lot of people can with a machine shop.
American proverb, mid 20th century.

Fall seven times, stand up eight.
Japanese proverb; compare **If at first you don't succeed, try, try, try again** below.

He that will to Cupar maun to Cupar.
if someone is determined on an end they will not be dissuaded (*Cupar* is a town in Fife, Scotland); Scottish traditional saying, early 18th century.

He who wills the end, wills the means.
someone sufficiently determined upon an outcome will also be ready to accept whatever is necessary to achieve it; English proverb, late 17th century.

If at first you don't succeed, try, try, try again.
English proverb, mid 19th century; compare **Fall seven times, stand up eight** above.

It is idle to swallow the cow and choke on the tail.
when a serious matter has been accepted, there is no point in quibbling over a trifle; when a great task is almost completed, it is senseless to give up; English proverb, mid 17th century.

Determination

It's dogged as does it.

steady perseverance will bring success; English proverb, mid 19th century.

Just say no.

motto of the Nancy Reagan Drug Abuse Fund, founded 1985.

Little strokes fell great oaks.

a person of size and stature can be brought down by a series of small blows; English proverb, early 15th century.

Nil carborundum illegitimi.

cod Latin for 'Don't let the bastards grind you down', in circulation during the Second World War, though possibly of earlier origin.

Put a stout heart to a stey brae.

determination is needed to climb a steep ('stey') hillside; Scottish proverb, late 16th century.

Revenons à ces moutons.

an exhortation to stop digressing and get back to the subject in hand; French, literally 'Let us return to these sheep', with allusion to the confused court scene in the Old French *Farce de Maistre Pierre Pathelin* (*c.*1470).

The show must go on.

American proverb, mid 19th century.

Determination

Slow and steady wins the race.
from the story of the race between the hare and the tortoise, in Aesop's *Fables*, in which the winner was the slow but persistent tortoise and not the swift but easily distracted hare; mid 18th-century saying.

A stern chase is a long chase.
a *stern chase* is a chase in which the pursuing ship follows directly in the wake of the pursued; English proverb, early 19th century.

The third time pays for all.
success after initial failure makes up for earlier disappointment; English proverb, late 16th century.

We shall not be moved.
title of labour and civil rights song (1931), adapted from an earlier gospel hymn.

We shall overcome.
title of song, originating from before the American Civil War, adapted as a Baptist hymn ('I'll Overcome Some Day', 1901) by C. Albert Tindley; revived in 1946 as a protest song by black tobacco workers, and in 1963 during the black civil rights campaign.

Where there's a will there's a way.
anything can be done if one has sufficient determination; English proverb, mid 17th century.

A wilful man must have his way.

a person set on their own ends will disregard advice in pursuing their chosen course; English proverb, early 19th century.

Difference

See SIMILARITY AND DIFFERENCE

Discontent

See SATISFACTION AND DISCONTENT

Discoveries

See INVENTIONS AND DISCOVERIES

Dislikes

See LIKES AND DISLIKES

Dogs

See also CATS, HORSES

The idea of the dog as protector goes back to the Cave canem *of the classical world, and is reinforced by the Persian proverb,* The dog is a lion in his own house.

Doubt

Cave canem.
Latin, 'beware of the dog', deriving originally from the Roman satirist Petronius (d. 65), *'Canis ingens, catena vinctus, in pariete erat pictus superque quadrata littera scriptum "Cave Canem".'*

[A huge dog, tied by a chain, was painted on the wall and over it was written in capital letters "Beware of the dog."]

The dog is a lion in his own house.
Persian proverb.

A dog is for life, not just for Christmas.
slogan of the National Canine Defence League (now Dogs Trust), from 1978.

Love me, love my dog.
English proverb, early 16th century.

There is no good flock without a good shepherd, and no good shepherd without a good dog.
motto of the International Sheep Dog Society, said to derive from a Scottish proverb.

 # Doubt

See CERTAINTY AND DOUBT

Dreams

See also SLEEP

Apart from the warning from 19th-century America that
Dreams retain the infirmities of our character, *dreams are
traditionally seen as predictive, if they can be correctly
interpreted.*

Dream of a funeral and you hear of a marriage.
English proverb, mid 17th century.

Dreams go by contraries.
English proverb, early 15th century.

Dreams retain the infirmities of our character.
American proverb, late 19th century.

Morning dreams come true.
English proverb, mid 16th century, recording a
traditional superstition.

Those who lose dreaming are lost.
modern saying, said to be an Australian Aboriginal proverb.

To dream of the dead is a sign of rain.
traditional saying.

Dress

See also APPEARANCE

Dress may be important as protection from the elements (Ne'er cast a clout till May be out), *or as allowing us to make a good impression:* If you want to get ahead, get a hat.

Blue and green should never be seen.

traditional warning against wearing the two colours together.

Clothes make the man.

what one wears is taken by others as an essential signal of status; English proverb, early 20th century.

Dress for the job you want, not for the job you have.

modern saying, used especially in the context of interviews.

Fine feathers make fine birds.

beautiful clothes confer beauty or style on the wearer; English proverb, late 16th century.

If you want to get ahead, get a hat.

advertising slogan for the British Hat Council, 1965.

It takes 40 dumb animals to make a fur coat, but only one to wear it.

slogan of an anti-fur campaign poster, 1980s; sometimes attributed to the English photographer David Bailey (1938–).

Ne'er cast a clout till May be out.

warning against leaving off old or warm clothes until the end of the month of May (the saying is sometimes mistakenly understood to refer to hawthorn blossom or *may*); English proverb, early 18th century.

Nine tailors make a man.

literally, a gentleman must select his attire from a number of sources (later also associated with bell-ringing, with the *nine tailors* or *tellers* indicating the nine knells traditionally rung at the death of a man); English proverb, early 17th century.

Drink ✿

See also DRUNKENNESS, FOOD

Sayings about drink often emphasize the attractions or characteristics of a particular form of alcohol, whether it be beer, vodka, or whisky.

Alcohol will preserve anything but a secret.

American proverb, mid 20th century.

Don't ask a man to drink and drive.

British road safety slogan, from 1964.

Guinness is good for you.

reply universally given to researchers asking people why they drank Guinness; advertising slogan for Guinness, from *c*.1929.

Drunkenness

Heineken refreshes the parts other beers cannot reach.

slogan for Heineken lager, from 1975 onwards.

If you are cold, tea will warm you; if you are too heated, it will cool you; if you are depressed, it will cheer you; if you are excited, it will calm you.

modern saying, attributed to W. E. Gladstone (1809–98) since the mid 20th century.

I'm only here for the beer.

slogan for Double Diamond beer, 1971 onwards.

Today's rain is tomorrow's whisky.

modern Scottish saying.

Vodka is an aunt of wine.

Russian proverb.

 # Drunkenness

See also DRINK

Apart from the risks of becoming addicted (The drunkard's cure is to drink again), *there are other dangers in falling under the influence of alcohol:* When the wine is in, the wit is out.

The drunkard's cure is drink again.

American proverb, mid 20th century.

He that drinks beer, thinks beer.

warning against the effect of intoxication; English proverb, early 19th century.

There is truth in wine.

a person who is drunk is more likely to speak the truth; English proverb, mid 16th century (the saying is found earlier in Latin as *in vino veritas*).

When the wine is in, the wit is out.

when one is drunk one is likely to be indiscreet or to speak or act foolishly; English proverb, late 14th century.

Eating

See also COOKING, FOOD, HEALTH

In the 21st century, the saying You are what you eat *has gained a new prominence, but earlier proverbs may be more likely to reflect a world in which eating was not something to be taken for granted:* Hunger is the best sauce.

After dinner rest a while, after supper walk a mile.

the implication is that dinner is a heavy meal, while supper is a light one; English proverb, late 16th century.

After meat, mustard.

traditional comment on some essential ingredient which is brought too late to be of use; English proverb, late 16th century.

Breakfast like a king, lunch like a prince, and dine like a pauper.

modern saying, recommending lighter meals as you move through the day.

Eat to live, not live to eat.

distinguishing between necessity and indulgence; English proverb, late 14th century.

Fingers were made before forks.

commonly used as a polite excuse for eating with one's hands at table; English proverb, mid 18th century; the earlier variant 'God made hands before knives is found in the mid 16th century.

Go to work on an egg.

advertising slogan for the British Egg Marketing Board, from 1957; perhaps written by Fay Weldon or Mary Gowing.

Hunger is the best sauce.

food which is needed will be received most readily; English proverb, early 16th century.

The way one eats is the way one works.

Czech proverb; compare **You are what you eat** below.

We must eat a peck of dirt before we die.

often used as a consolatory remark in literal contexts; English proverb, mid 18th century.

You are what you eat.

English proverb, mid 20th century; in the early 19th century, the French jurist and gourmet Anthelme Brillat-Savarin (1755–1826) wrote, 'Tell me what you eat and I will tell you what you are'; compare **The way one eats is the way one works** above.

Education

See also KNOWLEDGE, TEACHING

The saying As the twig is bent, so is the tree inclined *reflects an awareness of the importance of early influences, but for late developers there is the encouragement,* It is never too late to learn.

As the twig is bent, so is the tree inclined.

early influences have a permanent effect; English proverb, early 18th century.

Education doesn't come by bumping your head against the school house.

American proverb, mid 20th century.

Genius without education is like silver in the mine.

American proverb, mid 18th century.

Give me a child for the first seven years, and you may do what you like with him afterwards.

traditionally regarded as a Jesuit maxim; recorded in Lean's *Collectanea* vol. 3 (1903).

The ink of a scholar is holier than the blood of a martyr.

modern saying, said to derive from an Arab proverb, but of uncertain origin.

It is never too late to learn.

English proverb, late 17th century.

Never let your education interfere with your intelligence.

American proverb, mid 20th century.

Never too old to learn.

English proverb, late 16th century.

Teachers open the door, but you must enter by yourself.

learning requires effort on the part of the student; Chinese proverb.

There is no royal road to learning.

English proverb, early 19th century, deriving from the words of the Greek mathematician Euclid (fl. *c.*300 BC) addressed to Ptolemy I of Egypt, 'There is no "royal road" to geometry.'

When the pupil is ready, the master arrives.

Indian proverb, deriving from Sanskrit.

Effort

See also ACHIEVEMENT

Proverbs such as He that would eat the fruit must climb the tree *and* No pain, no gain *emphasize how*

Effort

essential effort is to achievement. There is comparatively little concern that the effort might be expended ineffectually, although by implication we are warned to set our sights on an achievable goal: If the sky falls, we shall catch larks.

Easy come, easy go.
something which is acquired without effort will be lost without regret; English proverb, mid 17th century.

He that would eat the fruit must climb the tree.
someone who wishes to attain success must first make the necessary effort; English proverb, mid 17th century.

If a thing's worth doing, it's worth doing well.
if something is worth any effort at all, it should be taken seriously; English proverb, mid 18th century.

If the sky falls we shall catch larks.
used dismissively to indicate that something will be attainable only in the most unlikely circumstances; English proverb, mid 15th century.

Much cry and little wool.
referring to a disturbance without tangible result; in early usage, the image was that of shearing a pig, which would cry loudly but yield no wool; English proverb, late 15th century.

No pain, no gain.

nothing worth having can be achieved without effort;
English proverb, late 16th century.

**One cannot become a good sailor sailing in a
tranquil sea.**

a person must be disciplined and educated to become a
useful citizen; Chinese proverb.

We're number two. We try harder.

advertising slogan for Avis car rentals.

Employment ❀

See also MANAGEMENT

*One saying from the 18th century and one saying from
the 20th offer very different views of employment: the
belief that* The eye of a master does more work than
both his hands *contrasts with the cynical comment
from Soviet Russia:* We pretend to work, and they
pretend to pay us.

**The eye of a master does more work than both
his hands.**

employees work harder when the person who is in charge is
present; English proverb, mid 18th century.

Ending

Jack of all trades and master of none.
a person who tries to master too many skills will learn none of them properly; English proverb, early 17th century.

We pretend to work, and they pretend to pay us.
Russian saying of the Soviet era.

✸ Ending

See also BEGINNING, CHANGE

Whether or not an ending is as successful as that implied by The end crowns the work, *it will inevitably arrive. However, we should not assume too quickly that something has been completed:* The opera isn't over till the fat lady sings.

All good things must come to an end.
nothing lasts; although the addition of 'good' is a later development; English proverb, mid 15th century.

All's well that ends well.
often used with the implication that difficulties have been successfully negotiated; English proverb, late 14th century.

And they all lived happily ever after.
traditional ending for a fairy story.

Better an end with terror than terror without end.

20th-century German saying, associated with Philipp Scheidermann (1865–1939), second head of government in the Weimar Republic.

The end crowns the work.

the fulfilment of a process is its finest and most notable part; English proverb, early 16th century.

End good, all good.

a good outcome means that the work has been worthwhile; German proverb.

Everything has an end.

no condition lasts for ever; English proverb, late 14th century.

In my end is my beginning.

motto of Mary, Queen of Scots (1542–87).

The opera isn't over till the fat lady sings.

using an informal description of the culmination of a traditional opera to indicate that a process is not yet complete; late 20th century saying.

Enemies

See also DANGER

While we should be cautious in our dealings with an enemy (Do not call a wolf to help you against the dogs), *shared enmity can be useful:* The enemy of my enemy is my friend.

Dead men don't bite.

killing an enemy puts an end to any threat they may pose; English proverb, mid 16th century.

Do not call a wolf to help you against the dogs.

advising against making alliance with someone likely to destroy you in your turn; Russian proverb.

The enemy of my enemy is my friend.

shared enmity provides common ground; American proverb, mid 20th century, often said to be 'an old Arab proverb'; compare **My brother and I against my cousin and my cousin and I against the stranger** at FAMILY.

Love your enemy—but don't put a gun in his hand.

indicating the practical limitations of charity; American proverb, mid 20th century.

Strike the serpent's head with your enemy's hand.

use one opponent to defeat another; English proverb.

There is no little enemy.
any enemy can be dangerous; English proverb, mid
17th century.

The Environment ❀

In recent years political slogans such as Think globally,
act locally *and sayings believed to derive from cultures
in touch with a pre-industrial way of living such as*
Touch the earth lightly *have combined to urge
sensitivity and care in dealing with the natural world.*

The earth is man's only friend.
Bulgarian proverb.

The earth laughs at him who calls a place his own.
Indian proverb.

**However high a bird may soar, it seeks its
food on earth.**
Danish proverb.

Save the whale.
environmental slogan associated with the alarm over the
rapidly declining whale population which led in 1985 to a
moratorium on commercial whaling.

The Environment

Take only photos, leave only footprints.

encouraging responsible behaviour when travelling in wilderness areas; mid 20th-century saying, first found as 'Take nothing but pictures; leave nothing but footprints', and often attributed to Chief Seattle (1786–1866) of the Suquamish and Duwamish in the form 'Take only memories, leave only footprints.'

Think globally, act locally.

Friends of the Earth slogan, *c.*1985.

Touch the earth lightly.

modern saying, said to derive from an Australian Aboriginal proverb.

We do not inherit the earth from our parents, we borrow it from our children.

modern saying, said to be of Native American origin.

When the last tree is cut, the last river poisoned, and the last fish dead, we will discover that we can't eat money.

Canadian saying, sometimes said to be of Native American origin.

You have to be in the black to be in the green.

a landowner who is in debt is more likely to damage the environment; modern New Zealand saying.

Envy

While being envied may sustain our pride, to feel envy is likely to make us discontented: The grass is always greener on the other side of the fence.

Better be envied than pitied.
even if one is unhappy it is preferable to be rich and powerful rather than poor and vulnerable; English proverb, mid 16th century.

Envy eats nothing but its own heart.
German proverb.

Envy feeds on the living; it ceases when they are dead.
American proverb, mid 20th century.

The grass is always greener on the other side of the fence.
something just out of reach always appears more desirable than what one already has; English proverb, mid 20th century.

If envy were a fever, all the world would be ill.
Envy is a common vice; Danish proverb.

Equality

An idea expressed through several images.

After the game, the king and the pawn go into the same box.

rank is no protection against death; Italian proverb.

Diamond cuts diamond.

used of persons who are evenly matched in wit or cunning (only a diamond is hard enough to cut another diamond); English proverb, early 17th century.

Jack is as good as his master.

'Jack' is used variously as a familiar name for a sailor, a member of the common people, a serving man, and one who does odd jobs; English proverb, early 18th century.

 # Evil

See GOOD AND EVIL

 # Excellence

True excellence may be seldom encountered, since If something sounds too good to be true, it probably is.

Corruption of the best becomes the worst.

translation of the Latin saying *Corruptio optimi pessima*; English proverb, early 19th century.

If something sounds too good to be true, it probably is.

late 20th-century saying.

Excess

See also MODERATION

The idea that You can have too much of a good thing *occurs in many cultures, from the medieval English warning that* The pitcher will go to the well once too often, *to the Chinese* Do not add legs to the snake after you have finished drawing it.

Do not add legs to the snake after you have finished drawing it.

advising against making superfluous and undesirable additions; Chinese proverb.

Even nectar is a poison, if taken to excess.

too much of anything is inadvisable; Hindu proverb.

It is the last straw that breaks the camel's back.

the addition of one quite minor problem may prove crushing to someone who is already overburdened; English proverb, mid 17th century.

Excuses

The last drop makes the cup run over.
the addition of something in itself quite minor causes an
excess; English proverb, mid 17th century.

The pitcher will go to the well once too often.
one should not repeat a risky action too often, or push one's
luck too far; English proverb, mid 14th century.

You can have too much of a good thing.
excess even of something which is good in itself can be
damaging; English proverb, late 15th century.

 Excuses

See APOLOGY AND EXCUSES

 Experience

While there is no doubt that experience is worth having
(Experience is the father of wisdom), *it may be gained
at the cost of some unpleasantness:* A burnt child
dreads the fire.

Appetite comes with eating.
desire or facility increases as an activity proceeds; English
proverb, mid 17th century.

A burnt child dreads the fire.

the memory of past hurt may act as a safeguard in the future; English proverb, mid 13th century.

Experience is the best teacher.

sometimes used with the implication that learning by experience may be painful; English proverb, mid 16th century.

Experience is the comb which fate gives a man when his hair is all gone.

American proverb, mid 20th century.

Experience is the father of wisdom.

real understanding of something comes only from direct experience of it; English proverb, mid 16th century.

Experience keeps a dear school.

lessons learned from experience can be painful; English proverb, mid 18th century.

A fall into a ditch makes you wiser.

Chinese proverb.

Good soup is made in an old pot.

successful results are due to age and experience; French proverb.

Experience

Live and learn.

often as a resigned or rueful comment on a disagreeable experience; English proverb, early 17th century.

Once bitten, twice shy.

someone who has suffered an injury will in the future be very cautious of the cause; English proverb, mid 19th century; compare **Once bitten by a snake, a man will be afraid of a piece of rope for three years** at CAUTION.

Some folks speak from experience; others, from experience, don't speak.

American proverb, mid 20th century.

They that live longest, see most.

often used to comment on the experience of old age; English proverb, early 17th century.

Walking ten thousand miles is better than reading ten thousand books.

theoretical knowledge must be consolidated by practical experience; Chinese proverb; compare **Walking ten thousand miles; reading ten thousand books** at KNOWLEDGE.

You cannot catch old birds with chaff.

the wise and experienced are not easily fooled; English proverb, late 15th century.

You cannot put an old head on young shoulders.
you cannot expect someone who is young and inexperienced to show the wisdom and maturity of an older person; English proverb, late 16th century.

You should make a point of trying every experience once, excepting incest and folk-dancing.
20th-century saying, repeated by Arnold Bax in *Farewell my Youth* (1943), quoting 'a sympathetic Scot'.

Extravagance

See THRIFT AND EXTRAVAGANCE

Fact

See HYPOTHESIS AND FACT

Failure

See SUCCESS AND FAILURE

Fame

See also REPUTATION

Lasting fame is not easily achieved, since even if it is well founded, without a written record it may be forgotten: Brave men lived before Agamemnon.

Brave men lived before Agamemnon.

to be remembered the exploits of a hero must be recorded; English proverb, early 19th century, from Horace (65–8 BC) *Odes*, 'Many brave men lived before Agamemnon's time, but they are all, unmourned and unknown, covered by the long night, because they lack their sacred poet.'

Common fame is seldom to blame.

reputation is generally founded on fact rather than rumour; English proverb, mid 17th century.

If any man seek for greatness, let him forget greatness and seek truth.

American proverb, mid 20th century.

More people know Tom Fool than Tom Fool knows.

English proverb, mid 17th century; *Tom Fool* was a name given to the part of the fool in a play or morris dance.

A tall tree attracts the wind.

fame may make you the subject of hostile attention; Chinese proverb.

Familiarity

See also NEIGHBOURS

While it may be safer to stick with what you know
(Better the devil you know, than the devil you don't),
it may be difficult to recognize the virtues of the
familiar. Without the enchantment lent by distance,
Local ginger is not hot.

Better the devil you know than the devil you don't.

understanding of the nature of a danger may give one an advantage, and is preferable to something which is completely unknown, and which may well be worse; English proverb, mid 19th century.

Better wed over the mixen than over the moor.

it is better to marry a neighbour than a stranger (a *mixen* is a midden); English proverb, early 17th century.

Familiarity

Blue are the hills that are far away.

a distant view lends enchantment; English proverb, early 20th century.

Come live with me and you'll know me.

the implication is that only by living with a person will you learn their real nature; English proverb, early 20th century.

Familiarity breeds contempt.

we value least the things which are most familiar; English proverb, late 14th century.

If you lie down with dogs, you will get up with fleas.

asserting that human failings, such as dishonesty and foolishness, are contagious; English proverb, late 16th century (earlier in Latin).

Local ginger is not hot.

modern saying, said to derive from a Chinese proverb; compare **A prophet is not without honour save in his own country** below.

A man is known by the company he keeps.

originally used as a moral maxim or exhortation in the context of preparation for marriage; English proverb, mid 16th century.

No man is a hero to his valet.

English proverb, mid 18th century, found earlier in French, in a letter from the society hostess Mme Cornuel (1605–94).

A prophet is not without honour save in his own country.

English proverb, late 15th century, from the Bible (Matthew 13:57), 'A prophet is not without honour, save in his own country, and in his own house'; compare **Local ginger is not hot** above.

There is nothing new under the sun.

English proverb, late 16th century, from the Bible (Ecclesiastes 1:9), 'The thing that hath been, it is that which shall be; and that which is done is that which shall be done: and there is no new thing under the sun.'

The Family

See also CHILDREN, PARENTS

Proverbial wisdom on the subject of the family finds a consensus in the view that Blood will tell. *The idea is expressed in detail in the Chinese saying,* Dragons beget dragons, phoenixes beget phoenixes, and burglars' children learn how to break into houses.

The apple never falls far from the tree.

family characteristics will assert themselves; English proverb, mid 19th century.

The Family

Blood is thicker than water.
in the end family ties will always count; English proverb,
mid 19th century.

Blood will tell.
family characteristics or heredity will in the end be
dominant; English proverb, mid 19th century.

The child of a frog is a frog.
Japanese proverb.

Children are certain cares, but uncertain comforts.
emphasizing the continuing responsibility and anxiety of
parenthood; English proverb, mid 17th century.

**Dragons beget dragons, phoenixes beget phoenixes,
and burglars' children learn how to break into houses.**
Chinese proverb; see **Like father, like son** below.

I belong by blood relationship; therefore I am.
on the importance of family ties in one's sense of identity;
African proverb.

A large family, quick help.
those related to you will provide ready help in time of need;
Serbian proverb.

Like father, like son.
often used to call attention to similarities in behaviour;
English proverb, mid 14th century.

Like mother, like daughter.

English proverb, early 14th century; the ultimate allusion
is to the Bible (Ezekiel 16:44), 'As is the mother, so is
her daughter.'

My brother and I against my cousin and my cousin and I against the stranger.

Arab proverb; compare **The enemy of my enemy is my
friend** at ENEMIES.

The shoemaker's son always goes barefoot.

the family of a skilled or knowledgeable person are often the
last to benefit from their expertise; English proverb, mid
16th century.

The son of a duck floats.

Arabic saying.

Fate ✺

See also THE FUTURE

*Views on fate see it as unlikely to be altered by human
intervention:* Man proposes, God disposes. *The only
strongly contrary assessment is found in the modern
American saying,* Fate can be taken by the horns, like
a goat, and pushed in the right direction.

Fate

Every hog has its Martinmas.

everyone has their destiny; *Martinmas*, the feast of
St Martin, 11 November, was the season at which pigs
and other domestic animals were slaughtered before winter;
traditional saying.

**Fate can be taken by the horns, like a goat, and
pushed in the right direction.**

with sufficient determination one need not be a helpless
victim of fate; American proverb, mid 20th century.

Hanging and wiving go by destiny.

an expression of fatalism about the course of one's life;
English proverb, mid 16th century.

**If you're born to be hanged then you'll never
be drowned.**

used to qualify apparent good luck which may have an
unhappy outcome; English proverb, late 16th century.

Man proposes, God disposes.

often now said in consolation or resignation when plans
have been disrupted; English proverb, mid 15th century.

**The mills of God grind slowly, yet they grind
exceeding small.**

English proverb, mid 17th century; in its current form, it
derives from Henry Wadsworth Longfellow's translation of
Sinnegedichte by Friedrich von Logau, 'Though the mills of

God grind slowly, yet they grind exceeding small; Though with patience He stands waiting, with exactness grinds he all' (Von Logau's first line is itself a translation of an anonymous verse in Sextus Empiricus *Adversus Mathematicos*).

Sour, sweet, bitter, pungent, all must be tasted.
We have to experience both happiness and sadness in life; Chinese proverb.

What goes up must come down.
commonly associated with wartime bombing and anti-aircraft shrapnel, and often used with the implication that an exhilarating rise must be followed by a fall; early 20th-century saying.

What must be, must be.
used to acknowledge the force of circumstances; English proverb, late 14th century.

Fear

See also COURAGE, DANGER

A fearful person is likely to suffer from more than just the effects of the danger they fear: Cowards may die many times before their death.

Feelings

Cowards may die many times before their death.

English proverb, late 16th century; in this form, a
misquotation from Shakespeare *Julius Caesar* (1599)
'Cowards die many times before their deaths; /The valiant
never taste of death but once.'

Fear makes the wolf bigger than he is.

Fear exaggerates what we are afraid of; German proverb.

 # Feelings

See also LOVE

*Good feeling is seen as something without which there
can be little real enjoyment:* Better a dinner of herbs
than a stalled ox where hate is. *Beyond this, ill
will directed against another may rebound on the
perpetrator:* Curses, like chickens, come home
to roost.

**Better a dinner of herbs than a stalled ox
where hate is.**

simple food accompanied by goodwill and affection is
preferable to luxury in an atmosphere of ill will; English
proverb, mid 16th century, with allusion to the Bible
(Proverbs 15:17), 'Better a dinner of herbs where love is,
than a stalled ox with hatred therewith.'

Curses, like chickens, come home to roost.

ill will directed at another is likely to rebound on the
originator; English proverb, late 14th century.

Out of the fullness of the heart the mouth speaks.

overwhelming feeling will express itself in speech; English
proverb, late 14th century, originally with allusion to the
Bible (Matthew 12:34), 'Out of the abundance of the heart
the mouth speaketh.'

Sing before breakfast, cry before night.

warning against overconfidence in early happiness
presaging a reversal of good fortune; English proverb,
early 17th century.

Flattery

See PRAISE AND FLATTERY

Flowers

See also GARDENS

*Flowers are a natural source of enjoyment, but they
require nurturing and protection:* It is not enough
for a gardener to love flowers; he must also
hate weeds.

Food

All the flowers of tomorrow are in the seeds of today.

Indian proverb; compare **A seed hidden in the heart of an apple is an orchard invisible** at TREES.

It is not enough for a gardener to love flowers; he must also hate weeds.

American proverb, mid 20th century.

Say it with flowers.

slogan for the Society of American Florists, from 1917.

❀ Food

See also COOKING, DRINK, EATING

Some sayings focus on particular foodstuffs, as in the traditional warning Don't eat oysters unless there is an R in the month. *However, and more importantly, food is recognized as the most basic necessity:* No dinner without bread.

An apple pie without some cheese is like a kiss without a squeeze.

traditional saying, early 20th century.

Don't eat oysters unless there is an R in the month.

from the tradition that oysters were likely to be unsafe to eat in the warmer months between May and August.

Every pomegranate has one seed that has come from heaven.

Arabic proverb.

God never sends mouths but He sends meat.

used in resignation or consolation; English proverb, late 14th century.

A hungry man is an angry man.

someone deprived of a basic necessity will not be easily placated; English proverb, mid 17th century.

It's ill speaking between a full man and a fasting.

someone in need is never on good terms with someone who has all they want; English proverb, mid 17th century.

The more butter, the worse cheese.

the more cream used for butter, the less available for cheese; traditional saying.

No dinner without bread.

Russian proverb.

Of soup and love, the first is best.

Spanish proverb.

Twice-cooked cabbage is death.

Latin proverb.

Fools

Despite the hopeful note struck by the saying Fortune favours fools, *the consensus is that a foolish person is more likely to be unfortunate:* A fool and his money are soon parted.

Ask a silly question and you get a silly answer.

often used to indicate that the answer is so obvious that the question should not have been asked; English proverb, early 14th century.

Empty vessels make the most sound.

foolish and empty-headed people make the most noise; English proverb, mid 15th century.

A fool and his money are soon parted.

English proverb, late 16th century.

Fools build houses and wise men live in them.

a shrewd person chooses to save themselves trouble, and benefit from the effort expended by another; English proverb, late 17th century.

Fortune favours fools.

a foolish person is traditionally fortunate; English proverb, mid 16th century.

Never attribute to malice that which is adequately explained by stupidity.

modern saying, often known as 'Hanlon's razor'.

A wise man changes his mind, a fool never.

obstinacy is a mark of folly; Spanish proverb.

Foresight

See also THE FUTURE

Foresight is seen as desirable (Prevention is better than cure), *but hard to achieve—while conversely,* It's easy to be wise after the event.

The afternoon knows what the morning never suspected.

Swedish proverb.

He who can see three days ahead will be rich for three thousand years.

even limited foresight is of great value; Japanese proverb.

If a man's foresight were as good as his hindsight, we would all get somewhere.

American proverb, mid 20th century.

Forgiveness

It is easy to be wise after the event.
the difficult thing is to make a correct judgement without
the benefit of hindsight; English proverb, early 17th century.

**It's too late to shut the stable door after the horse
has bolted.**
preventive measures taken after things have gone wrong are
of little effect; English proverb, mid 14th century.

Nothing is certain but the unforeseen.
warning against an overconfident belief in a future
occurrence; English proverb, late 19th century.

Prevention is better than cure.
English proverb, early 17th century.

To know the road ahead, ask those coming back.
Chinese proverb.

❀ Forgiveness

See also CONSCIENCE, GUILT

Not only should we be ready to seek forgiveness (A fault
confessed is half redressed), *refusal to forgive is
associated with the likelihood that we have wronged
another:* Offenders never pardon.

Forgiveness

Charity covers a multitude of sins.

charity as a virtue outweighs many faults; English proverb, early 17th century.

A fault confessed is half redressed.

by confessing what you have done wrong you have begun to make amends; English proverb, mid 16th century.

Forgiving the unrepentant is like drawing pictures on water.

forgiveness is meaningless unless there is true repentance on the part of the offender; Japanese proverb.

Good to forgive, best to forget.

it is even better to forget that you have been injured than to forgive the injury; North American proverb, mid 20th century.

Never let the sun go down on your anger.

recommending a swift reconciliation after a quarrel; from the Bible (Ephesians 4:26), 'Be ye angry and sin not: let not the sun go down upon your wrath.'

Offenders never pardon.

the experience of having wronged someone often fosters a continuing resentment of the victim; English proverb, mid 17th century.

Friendship

To know all is to forgive all.
English proverb, mid 20th century; the idea is found earlier
in French, in Mme de Stael *Corinne* (1807), '*Tout
comprendre rend très indulgent* [To be totally understanding
makes one very indulgent].'

✿ Friendship

*Although the good intentions of our friends can
sometimes be a burden* (Save us from our friends),
we depend on having them: A friend in need is a
friend indeed.

**Be kind to your friends: if it weren't for them, you
would be a total stranger.**
American proverb, mid 20th century.

A friend in need is a friend indeed.
a *friend in need* is one who helps when someone is in need
or difficulty; English proverb, mid 11th century.

A friend to all is a friend to none.
traditional saying affirming the value of true friendship over
surface amiability.

Hold a true friend with both your hands.
real friendship is something to be cherished;
African proverb.

Life without a friend, is death without a witness.
friendship gives meaning to life; Spanish proverb.

The road to a friend's house is never long.
Danish proverb.

Save us from our friends.
the earnest help of friends can sometimes be
unintentionally damaging; English proverb, late
15th century.

Two is company, but three is none.
often used with the alternative ending 'three's a crowd';
English proverb, early 18th century.

Futility

See also ACHIEVEMENT

*There are a number of ways of invoking the picture of a
futile course of action, from* Dogs bark, but the caravan
goes on *to* You can't make a silk purse out of a sow's ear.

Dogs bark, but the caravan goes on.
trivial criticism will not deflect the progress of something
important; English proverb, late 19th century.

Do not push the river, it will flow by itself.
typifying pointless activity; Polish proverb.

Futility

Hot water does not burn down the house.

typifying ineffective action; African proverb.

In vain the net is spread in the sight of the bird.

a person who has seen the process by which someone
intends to harm them is unlikely to be in danger; English
proverb, late 14th century.

Sue a beggar and catch a louse.

it is pointless to try to obtain restitution from someone
without resources; English proverb, mid 17th century.

You cannot carry two watermelons in one hand.

typifying an attempted action that is bound to fail; modern
saying, said to be an Arabic proverb.

You cannot get a quart into a pint pot.

used of any situation in which the prospective contents are
too large for the container; English proverb, late 19th century.

You cannot get blood from a stone.

often used, as a resigned admission, to mean that it is
hopeless to try to extort money or sympathy from those
who have none; English proverb, mid 17th century.

You cannot make bricks without straw.

nothing can be made or achieved if one does not have the
correct materials; English proverb, mid 17th century, with
allusion to the Bible (Exodus) in Pharaoh's decree to the
taskmasters set over the Israelites in Egypt, 'Ye shall no

more give the people straw to make brick, as heretofore: let
them go and gather straw for themselves.'

You can put lipstick on a pig, but it will still be a pig.
superficial improvements will not alter the fundamental
structure; modern saying.

**You can put your boots in the oven but that doesn't
make them biscuits.**
modern American saying.

You can't make a silk purse out of a sow's ear.
inherent nature cannot be overcome by nurture; English
proverb, early 16th century.

You can't unscramble scrambled eggs.
the results of some actions cannot be undone;
modern saying.

The Future

See also FORESIGHT, THE PAST, THE PRESENT

*The future may be bright, but too much focus on it may
mean that we lose sight of what is actually happening:
There is no future like the present.*

Coming events cast their shadow before.
some initial effects indicating the nature of an event may be
felt before it takes place; English proverb, early 19th century.

The Future

He that follows freits, freits will follow him.
someone who looks for portents of the future will find
himself dogged by them (*freits* are omens); Scottish proverb,
early 18th century.

An inch ahead is darkness.
we have no knowledge of the future; Japanese proverb.

There is no future like the present.
American proverb, mid 20th century.

Today you; tomorrow me.
often used in the context of the inevitability of death to each
person; English proverb, mid 13th century.

Tomorrow is another day.
English proverb, early 16th century.

Tomorrow is often the busiest day of the year.
commenting on the tendency to put off necessary work;
Spanish proverb.

Tomorrow never comes.
used in the context of something which is constantly
predicted to be imminent, but which never comes; English
proverb, early 16th century.

You can have apricots tomorrow.
Arabic saying.

Games

See SPORTS AND GAMES

Gardens

See also FLOWERS

Gardening is seen as a source of joy, but also one that requires a good deal of attention, especially where keeping control of weeds is concerned: One year's seeding makes seven years' weeding.

The answer lies in the soil.
traditional gardening advice.

Dig for victory.
Second World War slogan, encouraging production of food in gardens and allotments.

A garden is never finished.
no true gardener ever feels their work is complete; modern saying.

If you would be happy for a week take a wife; if you would be happy for a month kill a pig; but if you would be happy all your life plant a garden.
the saying exists in a variety of forms, but marriage is nearly always given as one of the ephemeral forms of happiness; English proverb, mid 17th century.

157

Gardens

Life begins on the day you start a garden.
modern saying, claimed to be a Chinese proverb.

More things grow in the garden than the gardener sows.
some plants will appear as part of the natural process; Spanish proverb.

One year's seeding makes seven years' weeding.
the allusion is to the danger of allowing weeds to grow and seed themselves; English proverb, late 19th century.

Parsley seed goes nine times to the Devil.
parsley is often slow to germinate, and there was a superstition that it belonged to the Devil, and had to be sown nine times before it would come up; English proverb, mid 17th century.

Select a proper site for your garden and half your work is done.
Chinese proverb.

Sow corn in clay, and plant vines in sand.
Spanish traditional saying.

Sow dry and set wet.
seeds should be sown in dry ground and then given water; English proverb, mid 17th century.

Walnuts and pears you plant for your heirs.

both trees are tradionally slow growing, so that the benefit will be felt by future generations; English proverb, mid 17th century.

Generosity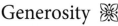

See also GRATITUDE

Generosity is seen as an obligation (It is better to give than to receive), *and one which should be readily fulfilled:* He gives twice who gives quickly.

Be kind. Everyone you meet is fighting a hard battle.

modern saying (sometimes misattributed to Plato).

A bird never flew on one wing.

frequently used to justify a further gift, especially another drink; early 18th-century proverb, mainly Scottish and Irish.

Friday's child is loving and giving.

English proverb, mid 19th century, from a traditional rhyme (compare qualities associated with birth on other days at entries under BEAUTY, SORROW, TRAVEL, and WORK).

Give a thing, and take a thing, to wear the devil's gold ring.

a school children's rhyme, chanted when a person gives something and then asks for it back; English proverb, late 16th century.

God

He gives twice who gives quickly.
associating readiness to give with generosity; English
proverb, mid 16th century.

It is better to give than to receive.
English proverb, late 14th century, ultimately with allusion
to the Bible (Acts 20:35), 'It is more blessed to give
than to receive.'

**It is easy to be generous with other
people's property.**
traditional saying, of classical origin.

 # God

While God may be omnipotent (All things are possible
with God)*, we are expected to make some efforts on
our own behalf:* God helps them that help themselves.

All things are possible with God.
English proverb, late 17th century, from the Bible (Matthew
19:26), 'With men this is impossible; but with God all
things are possible.'

God helps them that help themselves.
often used in urging someone to action; English proverb.

God writes straight with crooked lines.
God can use any instrument to achieve His ends;
Portuguese proverb.

The nature of God is a circle of which the centre is everywhere and the circumference is nowhere.

medieval saying, said to have been traced to a lost treatise of Empedocles; quoted in the *Roman de la Rose*, and by St Bonaventura in *Itinerarius Mentis in Deum*.

There's probably no God. Now stop worrying and enjoy your life.

slogan for a secular poster campaign on London buses, January 2009.

Good and Evil

See also VIRTUE

Although some goodness is unassailable (The sun loses nothing by shining into a puddle), *there is an insistence on the corrupting effects of evil:* He that touches pitch shall be defiled.

The greater the sinner, the greater the saint.

a sinner who has reformed is likely to be more virtuous that someone who is morally neutral; English proverb, late 18th century.

He that touches pitch shall be defiled.

a person who chooses to put themselves in contact with wrongdoing will be marked by it; English proverb, early

Good and Evil

14th century, with allusion to the Bible (Ecclesiasticus 13:1), 'He that toucheth pitch shall be defiled therewith.'

Honi soit qui mal y pense.

French, 'Evil be to him who evil thinks', the motto of the Order of the Garter, originated by Edward III, probably on 23 April of 1348 or 1349.

Ill weeds grow apace.

used to comment on the apparent success enjoyed by an ill-doer; English proverb, late 15th century.

Satan rebuking sin.

originally meaning that the worst possible stage has been reached; in later use, an ironic comment on the nature of the person delivering the rebuke; English proverb, early 17th century.

The sun loses nothing by shining into a puddle.

something which is naturally clear and radiant cannot be tainted or diminished by association; English proverb, early 14th century, of classical origin.

Two blacks don't make a white.

one injury or instance of wrongdoing does not justify another; English proverb, early 18th century.

Two wrongs don't make a right.

a first injury does not justify a second in retaliation; English proverb, late 18th century.

What is got under the Devil's back is spent under his belly.

what is gained improperly will be spent on folly and debauchery; English proverb, late 16th century.

Where God builds a church, the Devil will build a chapel.

the establishment of something which is itself good may also create the opening for something evil; English proverb, mid 16th century.

Gossip

While gossip may be seen as a natural part of human relations (Gossip is the lifeblood of society), it is more generally seen as likely to be damaging: according to the wartime security slogan, Careless talk costs lives.

Careless talk costs lives.

Second World War security slogan.

A dog that will fetch a bone will carry a bone.

someone given to gossip carries talk both ways; English proverb, early 19th century.

Give a dog a bad name and hang him.

once a person's reputation has been blackened his plight is hopeless; English proverb, early 18th century.

Gossip

Gossip is the lifeblood of society.
American proverb, mid 20th century.

Gossip is vice enjoyed vicariously.
American proverb, early 20th century.

The greater the truth, the greater the libel.
English proverb, late 18th century.

Loose lips sink ships.
American Second World War security slogan.

A tale never loses in the telling.
implying that a story is often exaggerated when it is
repeated; English proverb, mid 16th century.

Those who live in glass houses shouldn't throw stones.
it is unwise to criticize or slander another if you are
vulnerable to retaliation; English proverb, mid 17th century.

What the soldier said isn't evidence.
hearsay evidence alone cannot be relied on; English
proverb, mid 19th century, originally from Charles Dickens
Pickwick Papers (1837), 'You must not tell us what the
soldier, or any other man, said...it's not evidence.'

Whoever gossips to you will gossip about you.
a warning against enjoyment of gossip; Spanish proverb.

Government

See also POLITICS, SOCIETY

From the point of view of the subject, government is seen not only as powerful but also often as out of reach: God is high above, and the tsar is far away.

The cat, the rat, and Lovell the dog, rule all England under the hog.

contemporary rhyme referring to William *Catesby*, Richard *Ratcliffe*, and Francis *Lovell*, favourites of Richard III, whose personal emblem was a white boar.

Divide and rule.

government control is more easily exercised if possible opponents are separated into factions; English proverb, early 17th century.

God is high above, and the tsar is far away.

the source of central power is out of the reach of local interests; Russian proverb; compare **The mountains are high, and the emperor is far away** below, and **Delhi is far away** at CAUTION.

The mountains are high, and the emperor is far away.

the source of central power is out of the reach of local interests; Chinese proverb; compare **God is high above,**

and the tsar is far away above, and **Delhi is far away**
at CAUTION.

No fist is big enough to hide the sky.
there are limits to the powers of even the most repressive
regime; African saying.

✿ Gratitude

See also GENEROSITY

*The ungrateful person may discover too late the value of
what they have received:* You never miss the water till
the well runs dry.

The Devil was sick, the Devil a saint would be.
promises made in adversity may not be kept in prosperity;
English proverb, early 17th century.

Don't overload gratitude, if you do, she'll kick.
American proverb, mid 18th century.

Never look a gift horse in the mouth.
warning against questioning the quality or use of a lucky
chance or gift; referring to the fact that it is by a horse's teeth
that its age is judged; English proverb, early 16th century.

The river that forgets its source will dry up.
ingratitude brings its own punishment; African proverb.

When you drink water, remember who dug the well.

a warning against taking the efforts of others for granted; modern saying, said to be a Chinese proverb.

You never miss the water till the well runs dry.

applied to situations in which it is only when a source of support or sustenance has been withdrawn that its importance is understood; English proverb, early 17th century.

Greed

See also MONEY

When we give in to greed we are likely to find the appetite insatiable: Much would have more.

The more you get the more you want.

English proverb, mid 14th century.

Much would have more.

the ownership of substantial possessions creates in the owner the desire for still more; English proverb, mid 14th century.

Need makes greed.

Scottish proverb.

Guilt

Pigs get fat, but hogs get slaughtered.

used as a warning against greed; modern saying.

The sea refuses no river.

the sea's capacity is so great that anyone who chooses may
find a place there; English proverb, early 17th century.

**Where the carcase is, there shall the eagles be
gathered together.**

English proverb, mid 16th century, from the Bible (Matthew
24:28), 'Wheresoever the carcase is, there will the eagles be
gathered together.'

Guilt

See also CRIME AND PUNISHMENT

The experience of guilt is likely to be intolerable (The
guilty one always runs)*; we may as well* Confess
and be hanged.

Confess and be hanged.

guilt must be confessed and the due punishment accepted
for true repentance; English proverb, late 16th century.

The guilty flee when no man pursueth.

saying, with biblical allusion to Proverbs 28:1, 'The wicked
flee when no man pursueth; but the righteous are bold
as a lion.'

The guilty one always runs.

American proverb, mid 20th century.

Not guilty, but don't do it again.

comment on what is taken as a lucky escape from conviction; informal legal saying.

We are all guilty.

supposedly typical of the liberal view that all members of society bear responsibility for its wrongs; used particularly as a catchphrase by the psychiatrist 'Dr Heinz Kiosk', created by the satirist Peter Simple (pseudonym of Michael Wharton, 1913–2006).

We name the guilty men.

supposedly now a cliché of investigative journalism; *Guilty Men* was the title of a tract by Michael Foot, Frank Owen, and Peter Howard, published under the pseudonym of 'Cato', which attacked the supporters of the Munich agreement and the appeasement policy of Neville Chamberlain.

Habit

See CUSTOM AND HABIT

 # Happiness

See also HOPE

The unwise person will recognize happiness only when it is lost (Blessings brighten as they take their flight). An alternative way is to find reasons for happiness in unpromising circumstances: It is a poor heart that never rejoices.

Blessings brighten as they take their flight.

it is only when something is lost that one realizes its value; English proverb, mid 18th century.

Call no man happy till he dies.

traditionally attributed to the Athenian statesman and poet Solon (*c.*640–after 556 BC) in the form 'Call no man happy before he dies, he is at best but fortunate'; English proverb, mid 16th century.

A good time was had by all.

title of a collection of poems published in 1937 by Stevie Smith (1902–71), taken from the characteristic conclusion of accounts of social events in parish magazines.

Haste and Delay

Happiness is the only thing we can give without having.

modern saying.

Happiness is what you make of it.

American proverb, mid 19th century.

Hell is where heaven is not.

English proverb, late 16th century.

If I keep a green bough in my heart a singing bird will come.

we have some role in creating our own happiness;
Chinese proverb.

It is a poor heart that never rejoices.

often used to explain a celebratory action, and implying that
circumstances are not in general unrelievedly bad; English
proverb, mid 19th century.

Time flies when you are having fun.

modern saying, often in ironical usage.

Haste and Delay ✽

*While the hurried action associated with lack of
thought is likely to be ineffectual* (More haste, less
speed), *procrastination in itself is not an answer:*
Delays are dangerous.

Haste and Delay

Always in a hurry, always behind.
North American proverb, mid 20th century.

Delays are dangerous.
used as a warning against procrastination; English proverb, late 16th century.

Don't hurry—start early.
American proverb, mid 20th century.

Haste is from the Devil.
often used to mean that undue haste results in work being done badly or carelessly; English proverb, mid 17th century.

Haste makes waste.
hurried work is likely to be wasteful; English proverb, late 14th century.

Make haste slowly.
advising a course of careful preparation; English proverb, late 16th century; the idea is found in the classical world in the words of the Roman Emperor Augustus (63 BC–AD 14), 'Festina lente [Make haste slowly].'

More haste, less speed.
speed here meant originally 'success' rather than 'swiftness', and the meaning is that hurried work is likely to be less successful; English proverb, mid 14th century.

Never put off till tomorrow what you can do today.
English proverb, late 14th century.

Procrastination is the thief of time.
someone who continually puts things off ultimately achieves little; English proverb, mid 18th century, from Edward Young *Night Thoughts* (1742–5).

Health

See also EATING, MEDICINE, SICKNESS

The preservation of health is seen as lying in our own hands, though the medium of adopting a sensible lifestyle: Early to bed and early to rise, makes a man healthy, wealthy, and wise.

An apple a day keeps the doctor away.
eating an apple each day keeps one healthy; English proverb, mid 19th century; compare **Eat leeks in March and ramsons in May, and all the year after physicians may play** below.

Don't die of ignorance.
Aids publicity campaign, 1987.

Early to bed and early to rise, makes a man healthy, wealthy, and wise.
linking a healthy and sober lifestyle with material success; English proverb, late 15th century.

Health

Eat leeks in March and ramsons in May, and all the year after physicians may play.
ramsons = wild garlic; Welsh proverb; compare **An apple a day keeps the doctor away** above.

Eat till you're cold, live to grow old.
traditional saying.

Even your closest friends won't tell you.
advertising slogan for Listerine mouthwash, US, 1923.

Every good quality is contained in ginger.
Indian proverb.

Health is wealth.
traditional saying.

He who has health has hope; and he who has hope has everything.
Arabic proverb.

More die of food than famine.
American proverb, mid 20th century.

Slip, slop, slap.
sun protection slogan, meaning slip on a T-shirt, slop on some suncream, slap on a hat; Australian health education programme, 1980s.

Those who do not find time for exercise will have to find time for illness.

traditional saying.

Your food is your medicine.

Indian proverb.

History

To make a mark on history is not necessarily something to be sought: Happy is the country which has no history. *Beyond this, the objectivity of history is seen rather sceptically:* Until the lions produce their own historian, the story of the hunt will gratify the hunter.

Happy is the country which has no history.

memorable events are likely to be unhappy and disruptive; English proverb, early 19th century; compare a comment attributed to the French political philosopher Montesquieu (1689–1755) by Thomas Carlyle, 'Happy the people whose annals are blank in history-books!'

History is a fable agreed upon.

American proverb, mid 20th century.

History is fiction with the truth left out.

American proverb, mid 20th century.

The Home

History is written by the victors.
modern saying.

History repeats itself.
English proverb, mid 19th century.

Until the lions produce their own historian, the story of the hunt will glorify the hunter.
African proverb.

 # The Home

See also HOUSEWORK

There are various ways of expressing the importance of having a home, from East, west, home's best, *to the Chinese assertion that* Falling leaves have to return to their roots.

East, west, home's best.
English proverb, mid 19th century.

An Englishman's home is his castle.
a person has the right to refuse entry to his home; reflecting a legal principle, as formulated by the English jurist Edward Coke (1552–1634), 'For a man's house is his castle, *et domus sua cuique est tutissimum refugium* [and each man's home is his safest refuge]'; English proverb, late 16th century.

The Home

Every cock will crow upon his own dunghill.

everyone is confident and at ease on their home; English proverb, mid 13th century.

Falling leaves have to return to their roots.

everything must ultimately return to its origins; Chinese proverb.

Home is home though it's never so homely.

no place can compare with one's own home; English proverb, mid 16th century.

Home is where the heart is.

one's true home is wherever the person one loves most is; English proverb, late 19th century.

Home is where the mortgage is.

American proverb, mid 20th century.

Lang may yer lum reek!

long may your chimney smoke, often used as a toast; Scottish saying.

There's no place like home.

English proverb, late 16th century; the saying is found earlier in Greek, in the work of the Greek poet Hesiod (*c.*700 BC).

Honesty

See also CORRUPTION, DECEPTION, LIES, TRUTH

Honesty is essential in even the smallest actions (It's a sin to steal a pin), *although it is not always realistically to be expected* (Honesty is more praised than practised). *However, apart from moral duty there may be pragmatic reasons for adopting it:* Honesty is the best policy.

Children and fools tell the truth.

implying that they lack the cunning to see possible danger; tradition sometimes adds drunkards; English proverb, mid 16th century.

Confession is good for the soul.

confession is essential to repentance and forgiveness; English proverb, mid 17th century.

He who steals an egg will steal a camel.

someone who is guilty of petty dishonesty is likely to be guilty of more serious theft; modern saying, said to be an Arabic proverb.

Honesty is more praised than practised.

it is easier to advise another person to be honest than to be honest oneself; American proverb, mid 20th century.

Honesty is the best policy.

as well as being right, to be honest may also achieve a more
successful outcome; English proverb, early 17th century.

A howlin' coyote ain't stealin' no chickens.

American proverb, mid 20th century.

It's a sin to steal a pin.

even if what is stolen is of little value, the action is still
wrong; English proverb, late 19th century.

Nothing is stolen without hands.

if money or goods are missing, someone has stolen them;
English proverb, early 17th century.

Sell honestly, but not honesty.

a play on words meaning that honesty is the essential virtue
in commerce; American proverb, mid 20th century.

Hope

See also HAPPINESS, OPTIMISM AND PESSIMISM

Hope may make difficult circumstances bearable (If it
were not for hope, the heart would break), *but
over-indulgence in its promises will not lead to happiness:*
He that lives in hope dances to an ill tune.

Hope

Blessed is he who expects nothing, for he shall never be disappointed.

English proverb, early 18th century, originally with allusion to Alexander Pope (1688–1744), ' "Blessed is the man who expects nothing, for he shall never be disappointed" was the ninth beatitude.'

A drowning man will clutch at a straw.

when hope is slipping away one grasps at the slightest chance; English proverb, mid 16th century.

He that lives in hope dances to an ill tune.

hoping for something better may constrain one's freedom of action; English proverb, late 16th century.

Hope deferred makes the heart sick.

implying that it is worse to have had one's hopes raised and then dashed, than to have been resigned to not having something; English proverb, late 14th century, from the Bible (Proverbs 13:12), 'Hope deferred maketh the heart sick: but when the desire cometh, it is a tree of life.'

Hope is a good breakfast but a bad supper.

while it is pleasant to begin something in a hopeful mood, the hopes need to have been fulfilled by the time it ends; English proverb, mid 17th century.

Hope is the pillar of the world.

African proverb.

Hope springs eternal.

English proverb, mid 18th century, from Alexander Pope (1688–1744) *An Essay on Man* (1733), 'Hope springs eternal in the human breast: /Man never Is, but always To be blest.'

If it were not for hope, the heart would break.

referring to the role of hope in warding off complete despair; English proverb, mid 13th century.

In the kingdom of hope, there is no winter.

Russian proverb.

It is better to travel hopefully than to arrive.

often with the implication that something long sought may be disappointing when achieved; English proverb, late 19th century; from Robert Louis Stevenson *Virginibus Puerisque* (1881), 'To travel hopefully is a better thing than to arrive, and the true success is to labour.'

While there's life there's hope.

often used as encouragement not to despair in an unpromising situation; English proverb, mid 16th century.

Horses

See also CATS, DOGS

Sayings about horses reflect interests in choosing, and keeping, a horse, with an emphasis on personal

Horses

judgement and management: Care, and not fine
stables, makes a good horse.

Care, and not fine stables, makes a good horse.
Danish proverb.

No foot, no horse.
relating to horse care, and recorded in North America as 'no
hoof, no horse'; English proverb, mid 18th century.

**One white foot, buy him; two white feet, try him;
three white feet, look well about him; four white
feet, go without him.**
on horse-dealing, categorizing features in a horse which are
believed to be unlucky; English proverb, recorded in various
forms from the 15th century.

Pace makes the race.
from horse racing, relating to the setting of odds;
modern saying.

**There is nothing so good for the inside of a man as
the outside of a horse.**
recommending the healthful effects of horse-riding; English
proverb, early 20th century.

**The wind of heaven is that which blows between a
horse's ears.**
saying, said to be an Arabic proverb.

Hospitality

Hospitality is a natural source of enjoyment (It is merry in hall when beards wag all), *but guests can overstay their welcome. An African proverb recommends a way of dealing with this:* Treat your guest as a guest for two days; on the third day give him a hoe.

Always leave the party when you are still having a good time.

implying that pleasure of this kind is transient; American proverb, mid 20th century.

The company makes the feast.

the success of a social occasion depends on those present rather than on the food and drink provided; English proverb, mid 17th century.

The first day a guest, the second day a guest, the third day a calamity.

Indian proverb.

Fish and guests stink after three days.

one should not outstay one's welcome; English proverb, late 16th century.

Food without hospitality is medicine.

American proverb, mid 20th century.

Housework

A guest is like the morning dew.
a good guest does not stay very long; African proverb.

Hospitality and medicine must be confined to three days.
Indian proverb.

It is merry in hall when beards wag all.
when conversation is in full flow; English proverb, early 14th century.

The pot boils; friendship lives.
some friendships will not outlast the provision of hospitality; proverb of classical origin.

There isn't much to talk about at some parties until after one or two couples leave.
American proverb, mid 20th century.

Treat your guest as a guest for two days; on the third day give him a hoe.
African proverb.

✿ Housework

See also THE HOME

Apart from slogans promoting cleaning devices such as Hoover's It beats as it sweeps as it cleans, *sayings about housework tend to focus on it as the traditional sphere of activity for women:* A woman's work is never done.

He that will thrive must first ask his wife.
the husband's material welfare depends on the way in which his wife manages the household; English proverb, late 15th century.

It beats as it sweeps as it cleans.
advertising slogan for Hoover vacuum cleaners, 1919.

Persil washes whiter—and it shows.
advertising slogan for Persil washing powder, 1970s.

They that wash on Monday
Have all the week to dry;
They that wash on Tuesday
Are not so much awry;
They that wash on Wednesday
Are not so much to blame;
They that wash on Thursday
Wash for very shame;
They that wash on Friday
Wash in sorry need;
And they that wash on Saturday,
Are lazy folk indeed.
traditional rhyme.

The Human Race

A woman's work is never done.
reflecting the traditional responsibilities of the housewife;
English proverb, late 16th century.

✾ The Human Race

The view that Man is the measure of all things *can be traced back to the classical world, but later sayings suggest more of a limitation:* The best of men are but men at best, *or even the dialect summary,* There's nowt so queer as folk.

All mankind is divided into three classes: those that are immovable, those that are movable, and those that move.
modern saying, said to be an Arabic proverb.

Am I not a man and a brother?
motto on the seal of the British and Foreign Anti-Slavery Society, 1787, depicting a kneeling slave in chains uttering these words (subsequently a popular Wedgwood cameo).

The best of men are but men at best.
even someone of great moral worth is still human and fallible; English proverb, late 17th century.

God sleeps in the stone, dreams in the plant, stirs in the animal, and awakens in man.

traditional saying, frequently said to be of Indian origin; the wording varies in different languages.

Man is a wolf to man.

English proverb, mid 16th century, from the Roman comic dramatist Plautus (c.250–184 BC), 'A man is a wolf rather than a man to another man, when he hasn't yet found out what he's like.'

Man is the measure of all things.

everything could be understood in terms of humankind; English proverb, mid 16th century; found earlier in the classical world in the words of the Greek sophist Protagoras (b. c.485 BC), 'That man is the measure of all things.'

There's nowt so queer as folk.

English proverb, early 20th century.

What is the most important thing in life? It is people, people, people.

Maori proverb.

Young saint, old devil.

unnaturally good and moral behaviour at an early age is likely to change in later life; English proverb, early 15th century.

Hypothesis and Fact

See also SCIENCE, THINKING

While Facts are stubborn things, *they will not always be reached through speculation: the question* How many angels can dance on the head of a pin? *has become a type of fruitless hypothesis.*

The exception proves the rule.

originally this meant that the recognition of something as an exception proved the existence of a rule, but it is now more often used or understood as justifying divergence from a rule (compare **There is an exception to every rule** below); English proverb, mid 17th century.

Facts are stubborn things.

used to indicate a core of reality that cannot be adjusted to people's wishes; English proverb, early 18th century.

How many angels can dance on the head of a pin?

regarded satirically as a characteristic speculation of scholastic philosophy, particularly as exemplified by 'Doctor Scholasticus' (Anselm of Laon, d. 1117) and as used in medieval comedies.

Nullius in verba.

Latin, 'in the word of none', motto of the Royal Society, emphasizing reliance on experiment rather than authority; adapted from the Roman poet Horace *Epistles*, 'Not bound

to swear allegiance to any master, wherever the wind takes
me I travel as a visitor.'

One story is good till another is told.
doubt may be cast on an apparently convincing account by a
second told from a different angle; English proverb, late
16th century.

The proof of the pudding is in the eating.
the truth of an assertion will be demonstrated by how
things actually turn out; proof here means test'; English
proverb, early 14th century.

There is an exception to every rule.
English proverb, late 16th century; compare **The exception
proves the rule** above.

Idleness

See also ACTION AND INACTION, WORDS AND DEEDS

Idleness is not only seen as damaging and dangerous in itself (An idle brain is the devil's workshop), *it is not even necessarily enjoyable for the person who gives way to it:* Idle people have the least leisure.

As good be an addled egg as an idle bird.

an idle person will produce nothing; English proverb, late 16th century.

Better be idle than ill doing.

Scottish proverb.

Better to wear out than to rust out.

it is better to remain active than to succumb to idleness; in this form frequently attributed to Richard Cumberland, Bishop of Peterborough (1631–1718); English proverb, mid 16th century.

A day without work is a day without food.

modern saying, associated with Zen Buddhism.

The devil finds work for idle hands to do.

someone who has no work to do will get into mischief; English proverb, early 18th century.

Doing nothing is doing ill.

failing to do anything is effectively wrong-doing;
traditional saying.

An idle brain is the devil's workshop.

those who do not apply themselves to their work are most
likely to get into trouble; English proverb, early
17th century.

Idleness is never enjoyable unless there is plenty to do.

American proverb, mid 20th century; the idea is found in
the Jerome K. Jerome *Idle Thoughts of an Idle Fellow* (1886),
'It is impossible to enjoy idling thoroughly unless one has
plenty of work to do.'

Idleness is the root of all evil.

English proverb, early 15th century; the idea has been
attributed to the French theologian, monastic reformer, and
abbot St Bernard of Clairvaux (1090–1153); compare
Money is the root of all evil at MONEY.

Idle people have the least leisure.

lazy people are the least able to manage their time
efficiently; English proverb, late 17th century.

If you won't work you shan't eat.

essential sustenance is seen as a reward for industry; English
proverb, mid 16th century, from the Bible (II Thessalonians
3:10), 'If any would not work, neither should he eat.'

Ignorance

Who is more busy than he who has the least to do?
English proverb, early 17th century.

 Ignorance

Ignorance is not necessarily seen as an unhappy state:
Ignorance is bliss *from the 18th century finds an echo
from a Russian saying of the Soviet era,* The less you
know, the better you sleep.

The husband is always the last to know.
relating to marital infidelity; English proverb, early
17th century.

Ignorance is bliss.
English proverb, mid 18th century, from Thomas Gray *Ode
on a Prospect of Eton College* (1747), 'Where ignorance is
bliss,' Tis folly to be wise.'

Ignorance is voluntary misfortune.
one has chosen not to remedy the condition; American
proverb, mid 20th century.

It is dark at the foot of the lighthouse.
we often miss what is closest to us; Japanese proverb.

The last one to know about the sea is the fish.
the person with most reason to know about something often knows least; modern saying, claimed to be a Chinese proverb.

The less you know, the better you sleep.
Russian saying of the Soviet era.

Man is the enemy of that of which he is ignorant.
fear is a common response to the unknown; Arab proverb.

Nothing so bold as a blind mare.
those who know least about a situation are least likely to be deterred by it; English proverb, early 17th century.

A slice off a cut loaf isn't missed.
if someone has already been diminished or damaged, further damage may go unnoticed; English proverb, late 16th century (first recorded in Shakespeare's *Titus Andronicus*, 1592).

What the eye doesn't see, the heart doesn't grieve over.
now sometimes used with the implication that information is being withheld to prevent difficulties; English proverb, mid 16th century.

What you don't know can't hurt you.
English proverb, late 16th century.

Inaction

When the blind lead the blind, both shall fall into the ditch.

when a person is guided by someone equally inexperienced, both are likely to come to grief; English proverb, late 9th century, from the Bible (Matthew 15:14), 'They be blind leaders of the blind. And if the blind lead the blind, both shall fall into the ditch.'

 # Inaction

See ACTION AND INACTION

 # Indecision

See also CERTAINTY AND DOUBT

The consensus on indecision is that the person who cannot make a choice is likely to lose by it: Between two stools one falls to the ground.

Between two stools one falls to the ground.

inability to choose between, or accommodate oneself to, alternative viewpoints or courses of action may end in disaster; English proverb, late 14th century.

The cat would eat fish, but would not wet her feet.

commenting on a situation in which desire for something is checked by unwillingness to risk discomfort in acquiring it; English proverb, early 13th century.

Councils of war never fight.

people discussing matters in a group never reach the
decision to fight, which an individual would make; English
proverb, mid 19th century.

First thoughts are best.

advice to trust an instinctive reaction, often used as a
warning against indecision; English proverb, early
20th century.

He who hesitates is lost.

often used to urge decisive action on someone; English
proverb, early 18th century; early usages refer specifically to
women, as in Joseph Addison *Cato* (1713), 'The woman that
deliberates is lost.'

If you run after two hares you will catch neither.

one must decide on one's goal; English proverb, early
16th century.

Indecision is fatal, so make up your mind.

American proverb, mid 20th century.

Inventions and Discoveries

A theme which stresses the challenge of the new.

Inventions and Discoveries

Always something new out of Africa.

English proverb, mid 16th century; from the words of Pliny the Elder (AD 23–79), '*Semper aliquid novi Africam adferre* [Africa always brings [us] something new]', originally referring to the hybridization of African animals.

Do not follow where the path may lead. Go instead where there is no path and leave a trail.

late 20th-century saying, often attributed to Ralph Waldo Emerson (1803–82), but not found in his works.

Here be dragons.

alluding to a traditional indication of early map-makers that a region was unexplored and potentially dangerous.

If you don't make mistakes you don't make anything.

English proverb, late 19th century; the idea is found in a speech made at the Mansion House in London by the American lawyer and diplomat Edward John Phelps (1822–1900) on 24 January 1889: 'The man who makes no mistakes does not usually make anything.'

There is one thing stronger than all the armies in the world; and that is an idea whose time has come.

mid 20th-century saying; the idea is found in Victor Hugo *Histoire d'un Crime* (written 1851–2, published 1877),

'A stand can be made against invasion by an army; no stand can be made against invasion by an idea.'

Turkeys, heresy, hops, and beer came into England all in one year.

perhaps referring to 1521. The *turkey*, found domesticated in Mexico in 1518, was soon afterwards introduced into Europe; in 1521, the Pope conferred on Henry VIII the title Defender of the Faith, in recognition of his opposition to the Lutheran *heresy*; the *hop* plant is believed to have been introduced into the south of England from Flanders between 1520 and 1524; and *beer* as the name of hopped malt liquor became common only in the 16th century; English proverb, late 16th century.

Journalism

See NEWS AND JOURNALISM

 # Justice

See also CRIME AND PUNISHMENT, THE LAW

Fairness and honest dealing are desirable in themselves (Fair play's a jewel), *but beyond this there are serious consequences in making it difficult for anyone to obtain justice:* Justice delayed is justice denied.

All's fair in love and war.

in certain conditions rules do not apply, and any measures are acceptable; English proverb, early 17th century.

Be just before you're generous.

often used in the context of advising that one should settle any obligations before indulging in generosity; English proverb, mid 18th century.

A fair exchange is no robbery.

sometimes used of an action regarded as cancelling out an obligation which has been incurred; English proverb, mid 16th century.

Fair play's a jewel.

applauding the value of honest dealing; English proverb, early 19th century.

The fox should not be on the jury at the goose's trial.

a member of a jury must be unbiased; English proverb.

Give and take is fair play.

English proverb, late 18th century.

Give the Devil his due.

one should acknowledge the strengths and capabilities of even the most unpleasant person; English proverb, late 16th century.

Justice delayed is justice denied.

English proverb, late 20th century; compare a clause from Magna Carta (1215), 'To no man will we sell, or deny, or delay, right or justice.'

One law for the rich and another for the poor.

English proverb, mid 19th century.

There are two sides to every question.

a problem can be seen from more than one angle; English proverb, early 19th century.

Turn about is fair play.

recommending equality of opportunity; English proverb, mid 18th century.

We all love justice—at our neighbour's expense.

American proverb, mid 20th century.

Justice

What goes around comes around.
often used as a comment on someone becoming subject
to what they have visited on others; late 20th century,
of US origin.

What's sauce for the goose is sauce for the gander.
originally meaning that what is suitable for a woman is
also suitable for a man, but now sometimes used in wider
contexts; English proverb, late 17th century.

Knowledge

While knowledge is to be sought (The larger the shoreline of knowledge, the longer the shoreline of wonder, *and more simply* Knowledge is power), *we may be betrayed by over-confidence in our prowess:* A little knowledge is a dangerous thing.

The cobbler to his last and the gunner to his linstock.

the gunner's *linstock* was a long pole used to hold a match for firing a cannon, and the saying is a fanciful extension of **let the cobbler stick to his last** below; English proverb, mid 18th century.

Every picture tells a story.

advertisement for Doan's Backache Kidney Pills (early 1900s).

The good Christian should beware of mathematicians, and all those who make empty prophecies. The danger already exists that mathematicians made a covenant with the Devil to darken the spirit and to confine man in the bonds of Hell.

mistranslation of St Augustine's *De Genesi ad Litteram*, 'Hence, a devout Christian must avoid astrologers and all impious soothsayers, especially when they tell the truth, for fear of leading his soul into error by consorting with

Knowledge

demons and entangling himself with the bonds of such association' (the Latin word *mathematicus* means both 'mathematician' and 'astrologer').

I pointed out to you the stars and all you saw was the tip of my finger.
African proverb.

Knowledge and timber shouldn't be much used until they are seasoned.
American proverb, mid 19th century.

Knowledge is power.
English proverb, late 16th century, often with allusion to Francis Bacon *Meditationes Sacrae* (1597), 'Knowledge itself is power.'

The larger the shoreline of knowledge, the longer the shoreline of wonder.
North American proverb, mid 20th century.

Learning is a treasure that follows its owner everywhere.
reflecting on the advantage knowledge has over material possessions; Chinese proverb.

Learning is better than house and land.
reflecting on the difference between knowledge and material, and therefore ephemeral, possessions; English proverb, late 18th century.

Knowledge

Let the cobbler stick to his last.

people should concern themselves only with things they know something about (the cobbler's *last* is a shoemaker's model for shaping or repairing a shoe or boot); English proverb, mid 16th century; compare **The cobbler to his last and the gunner to his linstock** above.

A little knowledge is a dangerous thing.

English proverb, early 18th century; alteration of Alexander Pope *An Essay on Criticism* (1711), 'A little learning is a dangerous thing; Drink deep, or taste not the Pierian spring.'

One half of the world does not know how the other half lives.

often used to comment on a lack of communication between neighbouring groups; English proverb, early 17th century.

The sea of learning has no end.

Chinese proverb.

Straws tell which way the wind blows.

English proverb, mid 17th century.

There will be trouble if the cobbler starts making pies.

a warning against stepping outside one's area of expertise; modern saying, said to be a Russian proverb.

Knowledge

Walking ten thousand miles; reading ten thousand books.
theoretical knowledge and practical experience are of equal value; Chinese proverb, compare **Walking ten thousand miles is better than reading ten thousand books** at EXPERIENCE.

What's hit is history, what's missed is mystery.
on the importance of securing a dead specimen of a new species; late 19th century saying.

When a pine needle falls in the forest, the eagle sees it, the deer hears it, and the bear smells it.
modern saying, said to be of Native American origin.

When house and land are gone and spent, then learning is most excellent.
contrasting the value of learning with the ephemeral nature of material possessions; English proverb, mid 18th century.

The Law

See also CRIME AND PUNISHMENT, JUSTICE

The legal world is often seen as a perilous one (The more laws, the more thieves and bandits), *although not every saying goes as far as the Scottish proverb:* Home is home, as the Devil said when he found himself in the Court of Session.

The devil makes his Christmas pies of lawyers' tongues and clerks' fingers.

the lawyers' tongues and clerks' fingers stand for the words and actions of the legal profession as welcomed by the Devil; English proverb, late 16th century.

Gray's Inn for walks, Lincoln's Inn for a wall, The Inner Temple for a garden, And the Middle Temple for a hall.

on the four Inns of Court; traditional rhyme, mid 17th century.

Hard cases make bad law.

difficult cases cause the clarity of the law to be obscured by exceptions and strained interpretations; the saying may now also be used to imply that a law framed in response to a particularly distressing case may not be well thought out or well based; English proverb, mid 19th century.

The Law

Home is home, as the Devil said when he found himself in the Court of Session.
The *Court of Session* is the supreme civil tribunal of Scotland, established in 1532; Scottish proverbial saying, mid 19th century.

Ignorance of the law is no excuse for breaking it.
English proverb, early 15th century.

A man who is his own lawyer has a fool for his client.
English proverb, early 19th century.

The more laws, the more thieves and bandits.
a rigid and over-detailed code of law is likely to foster rather than prevent lawbreaking; English proverb, late 16th century; the idea is found in the *Tao-te Ching* of Lao Tzu (*c.*604–531 BC), 'The more laws and orders are made prominent, The more thieves and bandits there will be.'

No one should be judge in his own cause.
it is impossible to be impartial where your own interest is involved; English proverb, mid 15th century.

Possession is nine points of the law.
although it does not reflect any specific legal ruling, in early use the satisfaction of ten (sometimes twelve) points was commonly asserted to attest to full entitlement or ownership; possession, represented by nine (or eleven)

points is therefore the closest substitute for this; English proverb, early 17th century.

Rules are made to be broken.
English proverb, mid 20th century; the idea expressed by Christopher North in *Blackwood's Magazine* for May 1830, 'Laws were made to be broken.'

Where the law is uncertain, there is no law.
legal saying, late 18th century; earliest found in Latin *Ubi jus incertum, ibi jus nullum*.

Leadership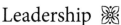

See also MANAGEMENT

While the health of an organization can be judged by that of its leadership (The fish always stinks from the head downwards), *there is also an awareness that a successful leader can also at need give loyalty and support to another:* A good leader is also a good follower.

As one fern frond dies, another is born to take its place.
Maori proverb, applied particularly to chiefs.

Equality is difficult, but superiority is painful.
on the difficulties of leadership; African proverb.

Leisure

The fish always stinks from the head downwards.
as the freshness of a dead fish can be judged from the condition
of its head, any corruption in a country or organization will be
manifested first in its leaders; English proverb, late 16th century.

A good leader is also a good follower.
American proverb, mid 20th century.

He that cannot obey cannot command.
the experience of being under orders teaches one how they
should be given; English proverb, late 15th century.

He who would lead must be a bridge.
Welsh saying.

If the people will lead, then the leaders must follow.
modern saying.

If you are not the lead dog the view never changes.
Canadian saying.

One mountain cannot accommodate two tigers.
there cannot be two leaders; Chinese proverb.

 # Leisure

See also IDLENESS, WORK

*Leisure is more than idleness in that it provides essential
refreshment:* All work and no play makes Jack a dull boy.

All work and no play makes Jack a dull boy.

warning against a lifestyle without any form of relaxation;
English proverb, mid 17th century.

The busiest men have the most leisure.

someone who is habitually busy is likely to make best use
of their time; English proverb, late 19th century.

Take time to smell the roses.

it is important to spend some time in leisure;
modern saying.

**The gods do not subtract from a man's allotted span
the time spent fishing.**

modern saying, sometimes claimed to have originated in an
Assyrian tablet.

Letters

Letters can be a key form of human communication:
A love letter sometimes costs more than a
three-cent stamp.

Do not close a letter without reading it.

American proverb, mid 20th century.

**A love letter sometimes costs more than a
three-cent stamp.**

American proverb, mid 20th century.

Lies

Someone, somewhere, wants a letter from you.
advertising slogan for the British Post Office, 1960s.

 # Lies

See also DECEPTION, HONESTY, TRUTH

Lies have their own power (A lie can go round the
world and back again while the truth is lacing up its
boots)*, but in the end a falsehood will be exposed:*
The liar's candle lasts till evening.

**An abomination unto the Lord, but a very present
help in time of trouble.**
definition of a lie, an amalgamation of lines from the Bible
(Proverbs 12:22, 'Lying lips are abomination to the Lord',
and Psalms 46:1, 'God is our hope and strength: a very
present help in trouble'), often attributed to the American
politician Adlai Stevenson (1900–62).

Even a liar tells the truth sometimes.
modern saying.

Half the truth is often a whole lie.
something which is partially true can still convey a
completely false impression; English proverb, mid
18th century.

A liar ought to have a good memory.

implying that one lie is likely to lead to the need for another;
English proverb, mid 16th century, 1st century AD in Latin.

The liar's candle lasts till evening.

a lie will be exposed sooner or later; Turkish proverb.

A lie can go around the world and back again while the truth is lacing up its boots.

American proverb, late 19th century; a variant is recorded
in the words of C. H. Spurgeon in *Gems from Spurgeon*
(1859), 'It is well said in the old proverb, "a lie will go round
the world while truth is pulling its boots on."'

One seldom meets a lonely lie.

implying that one is likely to lead to the need for another;
American proverb, mid 20th century.

To tell a falsehood is like the cut of a sabre, for though the wound may heal the scar will remain.

Persian proverb.

Life ✤

See also LIFESTYLES

While not necessarily easy (Life isn't all beer and
skittles), *the ultimate verdict is positive, if somewhat
bleak:* A live dog is better than a dead lion.

Life

Art is long and life is short.
originally from the Greek physician Hippocrates (*c*.460–357 BC), comparing the difficulties encountered in learning the art of medicine or healing with the shortness of human life ('Art' is now commonly understood in the proverb in a less specific sense); often quoted in the Latin version *Ars longa, vita brevis* from the rendering by the Roman philosopher and poet Seneca; English proverb, late 14th century.

Be happy while y'er leevin, For y'er a lang time deid.
Scottish motto for a house.

Life is a sexually transmitted disease.
graffito found on the London Underground.

Life is harder than crossing a field.
Russian proverb.

Life isn't all beer and skittles.
life is not unalloyed pleasure or relaxation; English proverb, mid 19th century.

Life is the best gift; the rest is extra.
African proverb (Swahili).

Life's a bitch, and then you die.
modern saying, late 20th century.

A live dog is better than a dead lion.

often used in the context of a lesser person taking the place of a greater one who has died; English proverb, late 14th century, from the Bible (Ecclesiastes 9:4), 'A living dog is better than a dead lion.'

Man cannot live by bread alone.

a person needs spiritual as well as physical sustenance; English proverb, late 19th century, after the Bible (Matthew 4:4), 'Man shall not live by bread alone, but by every word that proceedeth out of the mouth of God.'

Tout passe, tout casse, tout lasse.

French, meaning 'everything passes, everything perishes, everything palls'.

Lifestyles

See also LIFE

Common wisdom enshrines suggestions for essential principles by which to order our lives, from the simple Do as you would be done by, *to the Middle Eastern advice* If you have two coins, use one to buy bread, the other to buy hyacinths.

Lifestyles

Anyone can carry his burden, however heavy, until nightfall. Anyone can do his work, however hard, for a day. Anyone can live sweetly, patiently, lovingly, purely, till the sun goes down. And this is all that life really means.

traditional saying, late 19th century; associated with the writer Robert Louis Stevenson (1850–94) from the early 20th century.

Before enlightenment, chop wood, carry water. After enlightenment, chop wood, carry water.

Zen saying.

Do as you would be done by.

English proverb, late 16th century; in Charles Kingsley's *The Water Babies* (1863), Mrs *Doasyouwouldbedoneby* is the motherly and benevolent figure who is contrasted with her stern sister, Mrs *Bedonebyasyoudid*.

Do unto others as you would they should do unto you.

English proverb, early 10th century; from the Bible (Matthew), 'Therefore all things whatsoever ye would that men should do to you, do ye even so to them: for this is the law and the prophets.'

Eat, drink and be merry, for tomorrow we die.

a conflation of two biblical sayings, Ecclesiastes 8:15, 'A man hath no better thing under the sun, than to eat, and to drink, and to be merry', and Isaiah 22:13, 'Let us eat and drink; for tomorrow we shall die'; English proverb, late 19th century.

Fear less, hope more; Eat less, chew more; Whine less, breathe more; Talk less, say more; Love more, and all good things will be yours.

Swedish saying.

If you have two coins, use one to buy bread, the other to buy hyacinths.

both the mind and the body should be fed; Middle Eastern proverb (sometimes roses or lilies are suggested instead).

Make love not war.

student slogan, 1960s.

Likes and Dislikes

See also CRITICISM

From One man's meat is another man's poison *to* Tastes differ, *there is an acceptance that there is no consensus of personal preference.*

Every man to his taste.

often used to comment on someone else's choice; English proverb, late 16th century.

Losing

One man's meat is another man's poison.
pointing out that what may be necessary to one person is
injurious to another; English proverb, late 16th century.

One man's trash is another man's treasure.
modern saying.

Tastes differ.
different people will like or approve of different things;
English proverb, early 19th century.

There is no accounting for tastes.
often used in recognition of a difference in choice between
two people; English proverb, late 18th century.

You can't please everyone.
English proverb, late 15th century.

Losing
See WINNING AND LOSING

Love
See also MARRIAGE, RELATIONSHIPS

Love may be a powerful force (Love makes the world
go round), *but it does not necessarily bring ease:* The
course of true love never did run smooth.

The course of true love never did run smooth.

English proverb, late 16th century; originally from
Shakespeare *A Midsummer Night's Dream* (1595–6).

**It is best to be off with the old love before you are
on with the new.**

English proverb, early 19th century.

Jove but laughs at lovers' perjury.

English proverb, mid 16th century; from the Roman poet
Tibullus (c.50–19 BC) and ultimately from the Greek poet
Hesiod (c.700 BC).

Kissing goes by favour.

a kiss is often given as a reward for something done; English
proverb, early 17th century.

Love and a cough cannot be hid.

love can no more be concealed than a cough can be
suppressed; English proverb, early 14th century.

Love begets love.

English proverb, early 16th century.

Love is blind.

Cupid, the god of love, was traditionally portrayed as blind,
shooting his arrows at random, but the saying is generally
used to mean that a person is often unable to see faults in the
one they love; English proverb, late 14th century; compare
L'amour est aveugle; l'amitié ferme les yeux at RELATIONSHIPS.

Love

Love laughs at locksmiths.

love is too strong a force to be denied by ordinary barriers;
English proverb, early 19th century, from the title of a play
by George Colman the Younger (1762–1836).

Love makes the world go round.

English proverb, mid 19th century, from a traditional
French song.

Love makes time pass, and time makes love pass.

French proverb.

Love will find a way.

love is a force which cannot be stemmed or denied; English
proverb, early 17th century.

One cannot love and be wise.

English proverb, early 16th century; the statement 'to love
and be wise is scarcely allowed to God' is found in Latin in
the writings of the 1st-century Roman writer Publilius Syrus.

The quarrel of lovers is the renewal of love.

love can be renewed through reconciliation; English
proverb, early 16th century.

There are as good fish in the sea as ever came
out of it.

now often used as a consolation to rejected lovers in the
form 'there are plenty more fish in the sea'; English proverb,
late 16th century.

'Tis better to have loved and lost, than never to have loved at all.

English proverb, early 18th century.

When the furze is in bloom, my love's in tune.

with the implication that some furze can always be found in bloom; English proverb, mid 18th century; compare **When the gorse is out of bloom, kissing's out of fashion below.**

When the gorse is out of bloom, kissing's out of fashion.

the idea behind the saying is that gorse is always in flower somewhere (compare **When the furze is in bloom, my love's in tune** above).

Loyalty

Loyalty is a key virtue (It's an ill bird that fouls its own nest) *that is best demonstrated over a long period:* Quickly come, quickly go.

It's an ill bird that fouls its own nest.

a condemnation of a person who brings his own family, home, or country into disrepute by his words; English proverb, mid 13th century.

Luck

Love me little, love me long.
love of great intensity is unlikely to last; English proverb,
early 16th century.

Quickly come, quickly go.
English proverb, late 16th century.

 # Luck

See CHANCE AND LUCK

Management

See also EMPLOYMENT, LEADERSHIP

One traditional saying can be seen as an endorsement of the principle of delegation: Why keep a dog and bark yourself?

A committee is a group of the unwilling, chosen from the unfit, to do the unnecessary.

20th-century saying.

Hire slow, fire fast.

modern saying.

The nail that sticks up is certain to be hammered down.

Japanese proverb.

We trained hard . . . but it seemed that every time we were beginning to form up into teams we would be reorganized. I was to learn later in life that we tend to meet any new situation by reorganizing; and a wonderful method it can be for creating the illusion of progress while producing confusion, inefficiency, and demoralization.

late 20th-century saying, frequently (and wrongly) attributed to the Roman satirist Petronius Arbiter (d. AD 65).

221

Manners

Why keep a dog and bark yourself?

often used to advise against carrying out work which can
be done for you by somebody else; English proverb, late
16th century.

You cannot control the winds, but you can adjust the sails.

you may not be able to control matters, but you can respond
deftly to them; modern saying.

You can only manage what you can measure.

modern saying.

 # Manners

See also BEHAVIOUR

While courtesy is seen as an obligation (Manners
maketh man), *there is also a note of pragmatism:*
There is nothing lost by civility.

Civility costs nothing.

one should behave with at least minimal courtesy; English
proverb, early 18th century.

A civil question deserves a civil answer.

English proverb, mid 19th century.

Everyone speaks well of the bridge which carries him over.

someone is naturally well disposed towards a source of help, whether or not it has been beneficial to others; English proverb, late 17th century.

Manners maketh man.

motto of William of Wykeham (1324–1404), bishop of Winchester and founder of Winchester College; English proverb, mid 14th century.

Striking manners are bad manners.

American proverb, mid 20th century.

The test of good manners is being able to put up pleasantly with bad ones.

American proverb, mid 20th century.

There is nothing lost by civility.

English proverb, late 19th century.

Marriage

See also LOVE, MEN AND WOMEN, WEDDINGS

Despite the assertion that Marriages are made in heaven, *much proverbial wisdom takes a sceptical view of the happiness offered by the wedded state:* Needles and pins, needles and pins, when a man marries his trouble begins.

Marriage

Better be an old man's darling than a young man's slave.

English proverb, mid 16th century.

Better one house spoiled than two.

said of two wicked or foolish people joined in marriage; English proverb, late 16th century.

Change the name and not the letter, change for the worse and not the better.

it is unlucky for a woman to marry a man whose surname begins with the same letter as her own; English proverb, mid 19th century.

A deaf husband and a blind wife are always a happy couple.

each will remain unaware of drawbacks in the other (the saying is sometimes reversed to a blind husband and a deaf wife); English proverb, late 16th century.

The grey mare is the better horse.

the wife rules, or is more competent than, the husband; English proverb, mid 16th century.

Marriage is a lottery.

referring either to one's choice of partner, or more generally to the element of chance involved in how a marriage will turn out; English proverb, mid 17th century.

Marriages are made in heaven.

often used ironically; English proverb, mid 16th century.

Marry in haste and repent at leisure.

the formula is also applied to rash steps taken in other circumstances; English proverb, mid 16th century; the idea is found in William Congreve's play *The Old Bachelor* (1693), 'Thus grief still treads upon the heels of pleasure: / Married in haste, we may repent at leisure.'

Needles and pins, needles and pins, when a man marries his trouble begins.

traditional saying (originally a nursery rhyme), perhaps reflecting on the pressures of domestic life; English proverb, mid 19th century.

Never marry for money, but marry where money is.

distinguishing between monetary gain as a primary object and a side benefit; English proverb, late 19th century.

There goes more to marriage than four bare legs in a bed.

physical compatibility is not enough for a successful marriage; English proverb, mid 16th century.

Wedlock is a padlock.

English proverb, late 17th century.

A widow is a rudderless boat.

Chinese proverb.

Means

You do not marry the person you love, you love the person you marry.
Indian proverb.

A young man married is a young man marred.
often used as an argument against marrying too young;
English proverb, late 16th century.

 # Means

See WAYS AND MEANS

 # Medicine

See also SICKNESS

What drugs can do may be limited (The best doctors are Dr Diet, Dr Quiet, and Dr Merryman), *and some remedies may be in our own hands:* Laughter is the best medicine.

The best doctors are Dr Diet, Dr Quiet, and Dr Merryman.
outline of an appropriate regime for someone who is ill;
English proverb, mid 16th century.

Good ethics start with good facts.
modern saying in medical ethics.

Good medicine always has a bitter taste.

modern saying, sometimes claimed to be a Japanese proverb.

Keep taking the tablets.

supposedly traditional advice from a doctor, especially
when little change in the patient's condition is envisaged.

Laughter is the best medicine.

late 20th-century saying; the idea is an ancient one, as in
the Bible (Proverbs 17:22), 'A merry heart doeth good
like medicine.'

**Medicine can prolong life, but death will seize the
doctor, too.**

American proverb, mid 20th century.

Similia similibus curantur.

Latin, 'Like cures like,' motto of homeopathic medicine
attributed to S. Hahnemann (1755–1843), although not
found in this form in Hahnemann's writings.

Meeting and Parting

See also ABSENCE

While parting may be seen as a regrettable inevitability
(The best of friends must part)*, meeting is not
necessarily welcome:* Talk of the Devil, and he is
bound to appear.

Men

The best of friends must part.
no friendship is so close that separation is impossible; English proverb, early 17th century.

Nice to see you—to see you, nice.
catchphrase used by Bruce Forsyth in 'The Generation Game' on BBC Television, 1973 onwards.

Talk of the Devil, and he is bound to appear.
to speak of the Devil may be to invite his presence; often abbreviated to 'Talk of the Devil', and used when a person just spoken of is seen; English proverb, mid 17th century.

✳ Men

See also MEN AND WOMEN

Proverbial wisdom about men seems to be summed up in the succinct, Boys will be boys.

Boys will be boys.
English proverb, early 17th century, often used ironically.

I married my husband for life, not for lunch.
20th-century saying, origin unknown.

The way to a man's heart is through his stomach.
English proverb, early 19th century.

Men and Women

See also MARRIAGE, MEN, WOMEN

A loving partnership between men and women is seen as the natural pattern of life: Every Jack has his Jill.

Every Jack has his Jill.

all lovers have found a mate; English proverb, early 17th century.

A good Jack makes a good Jill.

used of the effect of a husband on his wife; English proverb, early 17th century.

A man is as old as he feels, and a woman as old as she looks.

both parts of the proverb are sometimes used on their own; English proverb, late 19th century.

The Mind

See also THINKING

The mind is seen as essential to independent life: Whom the gods would destroy, they first make mad.

A mind enlightened is like heaven; a mind in darkness is hell.

Chinese proverb.

229

Misfortunes

Mind has no sex.

modern saying, ultimately an alteration of the thought of Mary Wollstonecraft (1759–97) in her *A Vindication of the Rights of Women* (1792), 'To give a sex to mind was not very consistent with the principles of a man [Rousseau] who argued so warmly, and so well, for the immortality of the soul.'

A mind is a terrible thing to waste.

motto of the United Negro College Fund.

Our memory is always at fault, never our judgement.

American proverb, mid 20th century.

Whom the gods would destroy, they first make mad.

often used to comment on a foolish action seen as self-destructive in its effect; English proverb, early 17th century; the idea is found in the medieval period, in a scholiastic annotation to Sophocles's *Antigone*, 'Whenever God prepares evil for a man, He first damages his mind, with which he deliberates.'

✖ Misfortunes

See also ADVERSITY, CHANCE AND LUCK

Misfortunes are inevitable (The bread never falls but on its buttered side), *but we should not allow ourselves*

to be overwhelmed by a sense of our own bad luck:
I cried because I had no shoes, until I met a man
who had no feet.

Bad things come in threes.

the belief that an accident or misfortune is likely to be
accompanied by two more is traditional, although in this
form it is only recorded from the late 20th century.

The bread never falls but on its buttered side.

if something goes wrong, the outcome is likely to be as bad
as possible; English proverb, mid 19th century.

Help you to salt, help you to sorrow.

in which salt is regarded as a sign of bad luck (especially if
spilt at table); English proverb, mid 17th century.

I cried because I had no shoes, until I met a man who had no feet.

modern saying derived from a Persian original; compare
the words of the Persian poet Sadi (c.1213–91) in *The
Rose Garden,* 'I never complained at the vicissitudes of
fortune... excepting once, when my feet were bare, and
I had not the means of procuring myself shoes. I entered
the great mosque at Cufah with a heavy heart when I beheld
a man who had no feet. I offered up praise and thanks
giving to God for his bounty, and bore with patience the
want of shoes.'

Mistakes

If anything can go wrong, it will.

modern saying reflecting a supposed law of nature, said
to have been coined as a maxim in 1949 by George Nichols,
as the development of a remark made by a colleague,
Captain E. Murphy; the rule is popularly known as
'Murphy's Law'.

It is no use crying over spilt milk.

it is pointless to repine when it is too late to prevent the
misfortune; English proverb, mid 17th century.

It never rains but it pours.

if one thing has gone wrong, worse will follow; English
proverb, early 18th century.

Misfortunes never come singly.

English proverb, early 14th century.

 # Mistakes

*Not even the greatest expert can avoid making some
mistakes: we are warned that* Homer sometimes nods,
and Even monkeys sometimes fall off a tree.

Even monkeys sometimes fall off a tree.

even the most adept can be careless and make errors;
Japanese proverb.

He is always right who suspects that he makes mistakes.

warning against overconfidence; Spanish proverb.

He who slaps his own face should not cry out.

there is no point in complaining about trouble caused by your own error; Arabic proverb.

Homer sometimes nods.

even the greatest expert may make a mistake (nods here means 'becomes drowsy', implying a momentary lack of attention); English proverb, late 14th century, ultimately with allusion to the Roman poet Horace (65–8 BC), 'I'm aggrieved when sometimes even excellent Homer nods.'

A miss is as good as a mile.

if you miss the target, it hardly matters by how much; the syntax has been distorted by abridgement, and the original form was 'an inch in a miss is as good as an ell' (an *ell* being a former measure of length equal to about 1.1 metres); English proverb, early 17th century.

There's many a slip 'twixt cup and lip.

much can go wrong between the initiation of a process and its completion, often used as a warning; English proverb, mid 16th century.

Moderation

To err is human (to forgive divine).

English proverb, late 16th century (in its given form, from Alexander Pope's *An Essay on Criticism* (1711), 'To err is human: to forgive, divine'; compare **To err is human but to really foul things up requires a computer** at COMPUTERS.

Wink at sma' fauts, ye hae great anes yoursel.

avoid criticizing the mistakes of others, as you yourself have great ones; Scottish proverb; the idea is found in the Bible (Matthew 7:3), 'Why beholdest thou the mote that is in thy brother's eye, but considerest not the beam that is in thine own eye?'

✸ Moderation

See also EXCESS, GREED

Moderation is not only a sensible precaution against overindulgence (Enough is as good as a feast), *it can be positively beneficial in making an effect:* Less is more.

Enough is as good as a feast.

used as a warning against overindulgence, or overdoing something; English proverb, late 14th century.

Enough is enough.

originally used as an expression of content or satisfaction, but now more usually employed as a reprimand, warning someone against persisting in an inappropriate or excessive course of action; English proverb, mid 16th century.

The half is better than the whole.

advising economy or restraint; English proverb, mid 16th century, from the Greek poet Hesiod (fl. *c.*700 BC) *Works and Days,* 'the half is greater than the whole.'

Keep no more cats than will catch mice.

recommending efficiency and the ethic of steady work to justify one's place; English proverb, late 17th century.

Less is more.

something simple often has more effect; English proverb, mid 19th century.

Moderation in all things.

English proverb, mid 19th century, from the Greek poet Hesiod (fl. *c.*700 BC) *Works and Days,* 'Observe due measure; moderation is best in all things'; compare **There is measure in all things** below.

There is measure in all things.

English proverb, late 14th century; compare **Moderation in all things** above.

Money

See also THRIFT, WEALTH

It is natural to want money (Get the money honestly if you can), *but its power is in the end limited:* Money can't buy happiness.

Bad money drives out good.

money of lower intrinsic value tends to circulate more freely than money of higher intrinsic and equal nominal value, though what is recognized as money of higher value being hoarded; English proverb, early 20th century; known as 'Gresham's law' from Thomas Gresham (d. 1579), English financier and founder of the Royal Exchange.

The best things in life are free.

English proverb, early 20th century, originally from the title ofa song (1927) by Buddy De Sylva and Lew Brown.

Cash is king.

modern saying, summarizing the position in a recession.

Get the money honestly if you can.

American proverb, early 19th century; the idea is found in the classical world, in the poetry of Horace (65–8 BC), 'If possible honestly, if not, somehow, make money.'

He that cannot pay, let him pray.

if you have no material resources, prayer is your only resort;
English proverb, early 17th century.

Money can't buy happiness.

English proverb, mid 19th century.

Money has no smell.

English proverb, early 20th century in this form, but
originally deriving from a comment made by the Roman
Emperor Vespasian (AD 9–79), in response to an objection
to a tax on public lavatories; compare **Where there's muck
there's brass** below.

Money is like sea water. The more you drink, the
thirstier you become.

possession of wealth creates an addiction to money;
modern saying.

Money isn't everything.

often said in consolation or resignation; English proverb,
early 20th century.

Money is power.

English proverb, mid 18th century.

Money is the root of all evil.

English proverb, mid 15th century, deriving from the Bible
(I Timothy 6:10), 'The love of money is the root of all evil';
compare **Idleness is the root of all evil** at IDLENESS.

Money

Money, like manure, does no good till it is spread.
English proverb, early 19th century; the idea is found earlier
in the *Essays* of Francis Bacon (1561–1626), 'Money is like
muck, not good except it be spread.'

Money makes the dog dance.
Spanish proverb.

Money makes the mare to go.
referring to money as a source of power; English proverb,
late 15th century.

Money talks.
money has influence; English proverb, mid 17th century.

Shrouds have no pockets.
worldly wealth cannot be kept and used after death; English
proverb, mid 19th century.

Time is money.
often used to mean that time spent fruitlessly on something
represents a real loss of money which could have been
earned in that time; English proverb, late 16th century.

Where there's muck there's brass.
dirty or unpleasant activities are also lucrative (brass here
means 'money'); English proverb, late 17th century;
compare **Money has no smell** above.

You cannot serve God and Mammon.

now generally used of wealth regarded as an evil influence;
English proverb, mid 16th century, ultimately from the
Bible (Matthew 6:24), 'No man can serve two masters... Ye
cannot serve God and mammon.'

Mourning

See also DEATH, SORROW

Mourning is inevitable and natural (Grief is the
price we pay for love), *but overindulgence in it is not a
sign of sincere feeling:* A bellowing cow soon forgets
her calf.

A bellowing cow soon forgets her calf.

the person who laments most loudly is the one who is
soonest comforted; English proverb, late 19th century.

Grief is the price we pay for love.

late 20th-century saying.

Let the dead bury the dead.

often used to mean that the past should be left undisturbed;
English proverb, early 19th century (see Matthew 8:22).

No flowers by request.

an intimation that no flowers are desired at a funeral.

Murder

You can shed tears that she is gone or you can smile because she has lived.

preface to the Order of Service at the funeral of Queen Elizabeth the Queen Mother, 2002.

 # Murder

Traditional sayings emphasize not only that murder cannot be concealed (Murder will out), *but also that it is likely to breed further killing:* Blood will have blood.

Blood will have blood.

killing will provoke further killing; English proverb, mid 15th century; in this form from Shakespeare *Macbeth* (1606), It will have blood, they say blood will have blood.'

Guns don't kill people; people kill people.

National Rifle Association slogan.

Killing no murder.

English proverb, mid 17th century, originally from the title of a pamphlet by Edward Sexby (d. 1658), 'Killing no murder briefly discourse in three questions', an apology for tyrannicide.

Murder will out.

the crime of murder can never be successfully concealed; English proverb, early 14th century.

Music

The world of music may offer great enjoyment, but it is not a shield from reality: we are told from the 17th century that Music helps not the toothache.

It takes seven years to make a piper.
Scottish proverb.

Music helps not the toothache.
English proverb, mid 17th century.

Why should the devil have all the best tunes?
commonly attributed to the English evangelist Rowland Hill (1744–1833); many hymns are sung to popular secular melodies, and this practice was especially favoured by the Methodists.

Names

Names enshrine the essence of individual identity: If the cap fits, wear it.

The beginning of wisdom is to call things by their right names.
modern saying claimed to be a Chinese proverb.

By Tre, Pol, and Pen, you shall know the Cornish men.
traditional saying, referring to the frequency of these elements in Cornish names; English proverb, mid 16th century.

If the cap fits, wear it.
used with reference to the assumed suitability of a name or description to a person's behaviour; English proverb, mid 18th century.

If the shoe fits, wear it.
one has to accept it when a particular comment is shown to apply to oneself; found mainly in the US; English proverb, late 18th century.

It is not what you call me. It is what I answer to.
African proverb.

Only the camel knows the hundredth name of God.

saying from Arab folklore; in Islam there are ninety-nine names for Allah (referred to as the ninety-nine names of God'), in the main taken or derived from the Koran.

Nature

See also THE ENVIRONMENT

Nature is seen as a powerful force beyond our control:
You can drive out nature with a pitchfork, but she keeps on coming back.

Nature abhors a vacuum.

English proverb, mid 16th century.

One for the mouse, one for the crow, one to rot, one to grow.

traditionally used when sowing seed, and enumerating the ways in which some of the crop will be lost, leaving the residue to germinate; English proverb, mid 19th century.

You can drive out nature with a pitchfork but she keeps on coming back.

English proverb, mid 16th century, from the Roman poet Horace (65–8 BC) *Epistles*, 'You may drive out nature with a pitchfork, but she will always return.'

Necessity

Necessity may accustom us to difficult choices
(Desperate diseases must have desperate remedies),
but it may also have possible benefits: Necessity
sharpens industry.

Beggars can't be choosers.

someone who is destitute is in no position to criticize what
may be offered; English proverb, mid 16th century.

Desperate diseases must have desperate remedies.

in a difficult or dangerous situation it may be necessary to
take extreme or risky measures; English proverb, mid 16th
century; compare **Exceptional times require exceptional
measures** below.

Even a worm will turn.

even a meek person will resist or retaliate if pushed too far;
English proverb, mid 16th century.

Exceptional times require exceptional measures.

modern saying; compare **Desperate diseases must have
desperate remedies** above.

Hunger drives the wolf out of the wood.

even the fiercest animal will be driven from shelter by acute
need; English proverb, late 15th century.

If the mountain will not come to Mahomet, Mahomet must go to the mountain.

used in the context of an apparently insoluble situation. The saying refers to a story of Muhammad recounted by Francis Bacon in his *Essays,* in which the Prophet called a hill to him, and when it did not move, made this remark; English proverb, early 17th century.

Make a virtue of necessity.

one should do with a good grace what is unavoidable; English proverb, late 14th century.

Necessity is the mother of invention.

need is often a spur to the creative process; English proverb, mid 16th century.

Necessity knows no law.

someone in extreme need will disregard rules or prohibitions; English proverb, late 14th century.

Necessity sharpens industry.

American proverb, mid 20th century.

Needs must when the devil drives.

used in recognition of overwhelming force of circumstance; English proverb, mid 15th century.

When all fruit fails, welcome haws.

often used of someone taking of necessity an older or otherwise unsuitable lover *(haws,* the red fruit of the

hawthorn, are contrasted with fruits generally eaten as
food); English proverb, early 18th century.

Who says A must say B.
only recorded in English from North American sources,
and meaning that if a first step is taken; the second will
inevitably follow; English proverb, mid 19th century.

 # Neighbours

See also FAMILIARITY, FRIENDSHIP

*Common wisdom advises care in not overstepping
limits with one's neighbours, both in terms of territory*
(Good fences make good neighbours) *and personal
intimacy* (You should know a man seven years before
you stir his fire).

Good fences make good neighbours.
this reduces the possibility of disputes over adjoining land;
English proverb, mid 17th century.

A hedge between keeps friendship green.
it is wise to have a clear boundary between neighbours;
English proverb.

Love your neighbour, but don't pull down your hedge.
do not let feelings of friendship lead you to act unwisely;
English proverb.

A wall between both best preserves friendship.

it is wise to have a clear boundary between neighbours;
Spanish proverb.

What a neighbour gets is not lost.

one is likely to benefit from the gain of a neighbour or
friend; English proverb, mid 16th century.

**You should know a man seven years before you stir
his fire.**

used as a caution against over-familiarity on slight
acquaintance; English proverb, early 19th century.

News and Journalism

The traditional view that Bad news travels fast *is
countered by an African saying:* One who sees
something good must tell of it.

All the news that's fit to print.

motto of the *New York Times,* from 1896; coined by Adolph
S. Ochs (1858–1935).

Bad news travels fast.

bad news is more likely to be talked about; English proverb,
late 16th century.

Light for all.

slogan of the *Baltimore Sun.*

News and Journalism

No news is good news.
often used in consolation or resignation; English proverb, early 17th century.

One who sees something good must tell of it.
African proverb.

Watch this space!
further developments are expected and more information will be given later; *space* = an area of a newspaper for a specific purpose, especially for advertising.

Opinion

See also ARGUMENT, THINKING

Independent ideas may be approved (Thought is free), but too great an affection for one's own views can degenerate into obstinacy: Those who never retract their opinions, love themselves more than they love truth.

He that complies against his will is of his own opinion still.

English proverb, late 17th century, from Samuel Butler *Hudibras* pt 3 (1680), 'He that complies against his will, Is of his own opinion still.'

So many men, so many opinions.

the greater the number of people involved, the greater the number of different opinions there will be; English proverb, late 14th century, from Terence (c.190–159 BC) *Phormio,* 'There are as many opinions as there are people: each has his own correct way.'

Those who never retract their opinions, love themselves more than they love truth.

American proverb, mid 20th century.

Thought is free.

while speech and action can be limited, one's powers of imagination and speculation cannot be regulated; English proverb, late 14th century.

249

Opportunity

Where there are two Jews, there are three opinions.
Jewish saying.

The wish is father to the thought.
one's opinions are influenced by one's wishes; English
proverb, late 16th century, from Shakespeare *2 Henry IV*
(1597), 'Thy wish was father, Harry, to that thought.'

Opportunity

While we may have many opportunities (The world is
one's oyster)*, we are warned that an opportunity
missed will not come again:* He that will not when he
may, when he will he shall have nay.

All is fish that comes to the net.
everything can be used to advantage; English proverb, early
16th century.

All is grist that comes to the mill.
all experience or knowledge is useful (*grist* is corn that is
ground to make flour); English proverb, mid 17th century.

A bleating sheep loses a bite.
opportunities may be lost through idle chatter; English
proverb, late 16th century.

Opportunity

Every crisis provides an opportunity.
often used as encouragement in facing difficult
circumstances; modern saying.

Every dog has his day.
everyone, however insignificant, has a moment of strength
and power; English proverb, mid 16th century.

**He that will not when he may, when he will he shall
have nay.**
if an opportunity is not taken when offered, it may well not
occur again; English proverb, late 10th century.

**If the camel once gets his nose in the tent, his body
will soon follow.**
an apparently insignificant opening is likely to lead to more
serious developments; Arabic proverb.

If you snooze, you lose.
it is advisable to stay alert to opportunities; modern saying.

It is good fishing in troubled waters.
a difficult situation offers opportunities to those prepared to
exploit it; English proverb, late 16th century.

It's not what you know, but whom you know.
American proverb, mid 20th century.

Opportunity

Make hay while the sun shines.
one should take advantage of favourable circumstances
which may not last; English proverb, mid 16th century.

The mill cannot grind with the water that is past.
an opportunity that has been missed cannot then be used;
English proverb, early 17th century.

No time like the present.
often used to urge swift and immediate action; English
proverb, mid 16th century.

**Opportunities look for you when you are
worth finding.**
North American proverb, mid 20th century; compare
**Opportunity never knocks for persons not worth a
rap** below.

**Opportunity never knocks for persons not
worth a rap.**
American proverb, mid 20th century.

Opportunity never knocks twice at any man's door.
a chance once missed will not occur again; English proverb,
mid 16th century.

**A person who misses his chance, and the monkey
who misses his branch, can't be saved.**
Indian proverb.

A postern door makes a thief.

referring to the opportunity offered by a back or side entrance; English proverb, mid 15th century.

Strike while the iron is hot.

one should take advantage of opportunity; the allusion was originally to the work of a blacksmith; English proverb, late 14th century.

Take the goods the gods provide.

one should accept and be grateful for unearned benefits; English proverb, late 17th century.

Time and tide wait for no man.

often used as an exhortation to act, in the knowledge that a favourable moment will not last for ever; English proverb, late 14th century.

When one door shuts, another opens.

as one possible course of action is closed off, another opportunity offers; English proverb, late 16th century.

When the cat's away, the mice will play.

many will take advantage of a situation in which rules are not enforced or authority is lacking; English proverb, early 17th century.

A wise man turns chance into good fortune.

traditional saying.

The world is one's oyster.
opportunities are unlimited; an *oyster* is seen as both a delicacy and a source of pearls. Perhaps originally with allusion to Shakespeare's *The Merry Wives of Windsor* (1597), 'The world's mine oyster, which I, with sword will open'; English proverb, early 17th century.

Optimism and Pessimism

See also HOPE

Adopting a positive attitude may be recommended (Turn your face to the sun, and the shadows fall behind you), *but we should beware of overconfidence:* Don't halloo till you are out of the wood.

All's for the best in the best of all possible worlds.
English proverb, early 20th century, from Voltaire *Candide* (1759), 'In this best of possible worlds... all is for the best.'

Another day, another dollar.
a world-weary comment on routine toil to earn a living, originally referring to the custom of paying sailors by the day, so that the longer the voyage, the greater the financial reward; American proverb, mid 20th century.

Optimism and Pessimism

The darkest hour is just before dawn.
suggesting that the experience of complete despair may mean that matters have reached the lowest point and may shortly improve; English proverb, mid 17th century.

Don't bargain for fish that are still in the water.
Indian proverb; compare **Don't sell the skin till you have caught the bear** below.

Don't count your chickens before they are hatched.
one should not make, or act upon, an assumption (usually favourable) which may turn out to be ill-founded; English proverb, late 16th century; compare **Chickens are counted in the autumn** at AUTUMN.

Don't halloo till you are out of the wood.
you should not exult until danger and difficulty are past (halloo means 'shout in order to attract attention'); English proverb, late 18th century.

Don't sell the skin till you have caught the bear.
do not act upon an assumption of success which may turn out to be ill-founded; English proverb, late 16th century (early versions have *lion* or *beast* in place of *bear*); compare **Don't bargain for fish that are still in the water** above.

Every cloud has a silver lining.
even the gloomiest circumstance has some hopeful element in it; English proverb, mid 19th century.

Optimism and Pessimism

God's in his heaven; all's right with the world.
English proverb, from early 16th century in the form 'God
is where he was'; now largely replaced by this poem from
Robert Browning *Pippa Passes* (1841), 'God's in his
heaven—All's right with the world!'

**If ifs and ands were pots and pans, there'd be no
work for tinkers' hands.**
traditional response to an over-optimistic conditional
expression, in which *ands* is the plural form of *and* = 'if';
English proverb, mid 19th century.

If wishes were horses, beggars would ride.
what one wishes for is often far from reality; English
proverb, early 17th century.

If you had teeth of iron, you could eat iron coconuts.
saying from Senegal.

It's an ill wind that blows nobody any good.
good luck may arise from the source of another's
misfortune; English proverb, early 17th century.

The sharper the storm, the sooner it's over.
the more intense something is, the shorter time it is likely to
last; English proverb, late 19th century.

Optimism and Pessimism

Turn your face to the sun, and the shadows fall behind you.

recommending a positive attitude; modern saying, said to derive from a Maori proverb.

When the axe came into the forest, the trees said 'The handle is one of us!'

relying for safety on a supposed link with a potential aggressor may offer a false hope; Russian proverb.

When things are at their worst they begin to mend.

when a bad situation has reached its worst possible point, the next change must reflect at least a small improvement; English proverb, mid 18th century.

Parents

See also CHILDREN, THE FAMILY

Pride and affection in one's child (Praise the child, and you make love to the mother) *may be associated with ambitions for the child's worldly success:* Parents want their children to become dragons.

A father is a banker provided by nature.
French proverb.

He who takes the child by the hand takes the mother by the heart.
Danish proverb.

It is a wise child that knows its own father.
a child's legal paternity might not reflect an actual blood link; English proverb, late 16th century.

A mother understands what a child does not say.
Jewish proverb.

My son is my son till he gets him a wife, but my daughter's my daughter all the days of her life.
while a man who establishes his own family relegates former blood ties to second place, a woman's filial role is not affected by her marriage; English proverb, late 17th century.

Parents want their children to become dragons.
parents want their children to be successful;
Chinese proverb.

Praise the child, and you make love to the mother.
English proverb, early 19th century.

Send the beloved child on a journey.
Japanese proverb.

To understand your parents' love, you must raise children yourself.
Chinese proverb.

When drinking water, remember the source.
advocating filial piety; Chinese proverb.

Parting ❈

See MEETING AND PARTING

The Past ❈

See also THE FUTURE, HISTORY, THE PRESENT

The past may represent something that cannot now be changed (The past at least is secure), *or which still has the power to affect the future:* The past is always ahead of us.

The Past

Old sins cast long shadows.
current usage is likely to refer to the wrong done by
one generation affecting its descendants; English proverb,
early 20th century.

The past always looks better than it was; it's only pleasant because it isn't here.
American proverb, late 19th century.

The past at least is secure.
American proverb, early 19th century.

The past is always ahead of us.
the past is a reminder of what has been and what may be;
Maori proverb.

Things past cannot be recalled.
what has already happened cannot be changed; English
proverb, late 15th century.

What's done cannot be undone.
English proverb, mid 15th century.

You have drunk from wells you did not dig, and been warmed by fires you did not build.
the present generation depends on those who have
gone before; modern saying, said to be of Native
American origin.

Patience

See also DETERMINATION, HASTE AND DELAY

Not only is patience recommended as in itself the right way to behave (Bear and forbear), *it promises ultimate satisfaction:* If you sit by the river long enough, you will see the body of your enemy float by.

All commend patience, but none can endure to suffer.

American proverb, mid 20th century.

All things come to those who wait.

often used as an adjuration to patience; English proverb, early 16th century.

Bear and forbear.

recommending patience and tolerance; English proverb, late 16th century.

Don't put the cart before the horse.

don't reverse the proper order of things; English proverb, early 16th century.

First thing first.

English proverb, late 19th century.

Hurry no man's cattle.

sometimes used as an injunction to be patient with someone; English proverb, early 19th century.

Patience

If you sit by the river long enough, you will see the body of your enemy float by.

advocating patience in the face of wrongs; modern saying, said to derive from a Japanese proverb.

I sit on the shore, and wait for the wind.

what is expected will arrive sooner or later; Russian proverb.

It is a long lane that has no turning.

commonly used as an assertion that an unfavourable situation will eventually change for the better; English proverb, mid 19th century.

The longest way home is the shortest way home.

not trying to take a short cut is often the most effective way; English proverb, mid 17th century.

The man who removes a mountain begins by carrying away small stones.

a major enterprise begins with small but essential tasks; modern saying, claimed to be a Chinese proverb.

Nothing should be done in haste but gripping a flea.

used as a warning against rash action; English proverb, mid 17th century.

One step at a time.

recommending cautious progression along a desired route; English proverb, mid 19th century.

Patience

Patience is a virtue.

often used as an exhortation; English proverb, late
14th century.

Rome was not built in a day.

used to warn against trying to achieve too much at once;
English proverb, mid 16th century.

Slow but sure.

sure here means 'sure-footed, deliberate'; English proverb,
late 17th century.

Softly, softly, catchee monkey.

advocating caution or guile as the best way to achieve an
end; English proverb, early 20th century.

There is luck in leisure.

it is often advisable to wait before acting; English proverb,
mid 19th century.

Time brings roses.

patience is likely to be rewarded; German proverb.

A watched pot never boils.

to pay too close an attention to the development of a desired
event appears to inhibit the result; English proverb, mid
19th century.

Peace

We must learn to walk before we can run.
a solid foundation is necessary for faster progress; English proverb, mid 14th century.

What can't be cured must be endured.
there is no point in complaining about what is unavoidable; English proverb, late 16th century.

Where water flows, a channel is formed.
success will come when conditions are right; Chinese proverb.

With time and patience the mulberry leaf becomes satin.
allowing time for a process to complete itself will be rewarded (silkworms feed chiefly on mulberry leaves); English proverb, late 17th century.

 # Peace

See also WARFARE

Peace may be desirable, but is perhaps only fully appreciated in contrast to strife: After a storm comes a calm.

After a storm comes a calm.
often used with the implication that a calm situation is only achieved after stress and turmoil; English proverb, late 14th century.

Ban the bomb.
US anti-nuclear slogan, 1953 onwards, adopted by the
Campaign for Nuclear Disarmament.

Nothing can bring you peace but yourself.
American proverb, mid 19th century.

**Peace is the dream of the wise; war is the history
of man.**
saying, recorded from the 19th century.

Pessimism

See OPTIMISM AND PESSIMISM

Politics

See also GOVERNMENT

*Sayings about politics can bring together a wide range
of views, perhaps exemplified in the words,* Politics
makes strange bedfellows.

**Are you now or have you ever been a member of the
Communist Party?**
formal question put to those appearing before the
Committee on UnAmerican Activities during the McCarthy
campaign of 1950–4 against alleged Communists in the

Politics

US government and other institutions; the allusive form *are you now or have you ever been?* derives from this.

As Maine goes, so goes the nation.
American political saying relating to presidential elections, *c*.1840.

Democracy is better than tyranny.
an imperfect system is better than a bad one; American proverb.

I am a Marxist—of the Groucho tendency.
slogan found at Nanterre in Paris, 1968.

In politics a man must learn to rise above principle.
American proverb, mid 20th century.

It'll play in Peoria.
catchphrase of the Nixon administration (early 1970s) meaning 'it will be acceptable to middle America', but originating in a standard music hall joke of the 1930s.

Lean liberty is better than fat slavery.
asserting that freedom matters more than any material comfort; English proverb, early 17th century.

Liberté! Égalité! Fraternité!
French, 'Freedom! Equality! Brotherhood!', motto of the French Revolution, 1789, but of earlier origin.

Not to be a republican at twenty is proof of want of heart; to be one at thirty is proof of want of head.

often used in the form 'Not to be a socialist…'; saying attributed to Georges Clemenceau (1841–1929) and to François Guizot (1787–1874).

The passion for freedom never dies.

saying, claimed to be a Greek proverb.

The personal is political.

1970s feminist slogan, coined by Carol Hanisch.

A politician is an animal who can sit on a fence and yet keep both ears to the ground.

American saying, mid 20th century.

Politics makes strange bedfellows.

political alliances in a common cause may bring together those of widely differing views; English proverb, mid 19th century.

Power to the people.

slogan of the Black Panther movement, from c.1968 onwards.

A straw vote only shows which way the hot air blows.

American proverb, early 20th century.

Possessions

Three acres and a cow.

regarded as the requirement for self-sufficiency; late 19th-century political slogan.

The voice of the people is the voice of God.

English version of the Latin *vox populi, vox dei*; English proverb, early 15th century; the Latin form is found in the writings of the English scholar and theologian Alcuin (*c.*735–804), 'And those people should not be listened to who keep saying the voice of the people is the voice of God, since the riotousness of the crowd is always very close to madness.'

Vote early and vote often.

American election slogan, already current when quoted by William Porcher Miles in the House of Representatives, 31 March 1858.

✿ Possessions

There is considerable emphasis on the idea of ensuring that you keep what you have (What you have, hold), *even if you do not immediately feel that it has a purpose:* Keep a thing seven years and you'll always find a use for it.

Finders keepers (losers weepers).

English proverb, early 19th century.

Findings keepings.

English proverb, mid 19th century.

If you have nothing, you have nothing to lose.

modern saying, claimed to be an Arabic proverb.

Keep a thing seven years and you'll always find a use for it.

recommending caution and thrift; English proverb, early 17th century.

Light come, light go.

something gained without effort can be lost without much regret; English proverb, late 14th century.

What you have, hold.

with reference to an uncompromising position based on a refusal to make any concession; English proverb, mid 15th century.

What you spend, you have.

the only real possessions one has are those of which one can dispose; English proverb, early 14th century.

You cannot lose what you never had.

used in consolation or resignation; English proverb, late 16th century.

Poverty

See also MONEY, WEALTH

Poverty can be destructive, both in sapping independence (Empty sacks will never stand upright) *and destroying relationships:* When poverty comes in at the door, love flies out of the window.

Both poverty and prosperity come from spending money—prosperity from spending it wisely.

American proverb, mid 20th century.

Empty sacks will never stand upright.

those in an extremity of need cannot survive; English proverb, mid 17th century.

Make poverty history.

slogan of a campaign launched in 2005 by a coalition of charities and other groups to pressure governments to take action to reduce poverty.

A moneyless man goes fast through the market.

someone without resources is unable to pause to buy anything (or, in a modern variant, rushes to wherever what they lack may be found); English proverb, early 18th century.

Poverty comes from God, but not dirt.

American proverb, mid 20th century.

Poverty is a blessing hated by all men.

poverty may shield you from worldly temptations, but it is
unpleasant to experience; Italian proverb.

**Poverty is no disgrace, but it's a great
inconvenience.**

English proverb, late 16th century.

Poverty is not a crime.

English proverb, late 16th century.

**When poverty comes in at the door, love flies out of
the window.**

the strains of living in poverty often destroy a loving
relationship; English proverb, mid 17th century.

Power ✺

The exercise of power may make someone predatory
(Big fish eat little fish), *but we should remember that
even an apparently weak person can be effective:* A
mouse may help a lion.

Better be the head of a dog than the tail of a lion.

it is preferable to be at the head of a small organization
than in a lowly position in a large one; English proverb,
late 16th century.

Power

Big fish eat little fish.
the rich and powerful are likely to prey on those who are less strong, often used with the implication that each predator is in turn victim to a stronger one; English proverb, early 13th century.

He who pays the piper calls the tune.
the person financially responsible for something can control what is done; English proverb, late 19th century.

Kings have long arms.
a king's power reaches a long way; English proverb, mid 16th century.

Might is right.
English proverb, early 14th century.

A mouse may help a lion.
alluding to Aesop's fable of the lion and the rat, in which a rat saved a lion which had been trapped in a net by gnawing through the cords which bound it; English proverb, mid 16th century.

Power corrupts.
English proverb, late 19th century.

Power is like an egg; if you hold it too tightly, it breaks, and if you hold it too loosely, it drops and breaks.
power should be exercised with proper attention, but without repression; African proverb.

Set a beggar on horseback, and he'll ride to the Devil.

a person unused to power will make unwise use of it; English proverb, late 16th century.

They that dance must pay the fiddler.

you must be prepared to make recompense for the provision of an essential service; English proverb, mid 17th century.

When elephants fight, it is the grass that gets hurt.

the weak are likely to suffer as a result of the conflicts of the strong and powerful; African proverb (Swahili).

When whales fight, the shrimp's back is broken.

Korean proverb.

Where the needle goes, the thread must follow.

Polish saying.

Practicality

See also CIRCUMSTANCE AND SITUATION

We should be ready to accept the limitations imposed by circumstances: Cut your coat according to your cloth.

A big fish is caught with a big bait.

African saying.

Praise and Flattery

Cut your coat according to your cloth.

actions taken should suit one's circumstances or resources;
English proverb, mid 16th century.

He who wants a rose must respect the thorn.

someone wanting a desirable object needs to be aware of the
dangers it brings with it; Persian proverb; compare **No rose
without a thorn** at CIRCUMSTANCE AND SITUATION and **Do not
grieve that rose trees have thorns, rather rejoice that
thorny bushes bear roses** at SATISFACTION.

The only part of a pig that can't be used is its squeak.

traditional saying.

Put your trust in God, and keep your powder dry.

often attributed to Oliver Cromwell (1599–1658); English
proverb, mid 19th century; compare **Trust in Allah, but tie
up your camel** at CAUTION.

You cannot make an omelette without breaking eggs.

often used in the context of a regrettable political necessity
which is said to be justified because it will benefit the
majority; English proverb, mid 19th century.

✻ Praise and Flattery

Praise that is well based is worth having (Praise from Sir
Hubert is praise indeed), *but flattery is worthless:*
Flattery, like perfume, should be smelled, not swallowed.

The cuckoo praises the rooster because the rooster praises the cuckoo.

Russian saying, based on Ivan Krylov's fable 'The Cuckoo and the Rooster' (1834).

Flattery is soft soap, and soft soap is ninety per cent lye.

distinguishing between soundly based compliment and insincere congratulation (*lye* is a strongly alkaline solution, especially of potassium hydroxide, used for washing or cleansing); American proverb, mid 19th century.

Flattery, like perfume, should be smelled, not swallowed.

American proverb, mid 19th century.

Give credit where credit is due.

English proverb, late 18th century.

Imitation is the sincerest form of flattery.

English proverb, early 19th century, from Charles Caleb Colton *Lacon* (1820).

Praise from Sir Hubert is praise indeed.

popular saying, a misquotation of a line from Thomas Morton *A Cure for the Headache* (1797), 'Approbation from Sir Hubert Stanley is praise indeed.'

Prejudice and Tolerance

While we should accept the views of others (Live and let live), *real prejudice is both unwelcome and difficult to eradicate:* No tree takes so deep a root as prejudice.

Judge not, that ye be not judged.

used as a warning against overhasty criticism of someone; English proverb, late 15th century, from the Bible (Matthew 7:1).

Live and let live.

often used in the context of coexistence between deeply divided groups; English proverb, early 17th century.

No tree takes so deep a root as prejudice.

emphasizing how difficult it is to eradicate prejudice; American proverb, mid 20th century.

There's none so blind as those who will not see.

used in reference to someone who is unwilling to recognize unwelcome facts; English proverb, mid 16th century.

There's none so deaf as those who will not hear.

used to refer to someone who chooses not to listen to unwelcome information; English proverb, mid 16th century.

Preparation and Readiness

Forethought is endorsed (The early bird catches the worm), *but we should not expend too much attention on circumstances that have not yet arisen:* Don't cross the bridge till you come to it.

Be prepared.

motto of the Scout and Guide organizations, deriving from the initials of Robert Baden-Powell (1857–1941), the founder.

Dig the well before you are thirsty.

make necessary preparations before you are in need; Japanese proverb.

Don't cross the bridge till you come to it.

warning that you should not concern yourself with possible difficulties unless and until they arise; English proverb, mid 19th century.

Don't throw away the old bucket, until you know whether the new one holds water.

do not get rid of a useful resource until you are sure that its replacement functions properly; Swedish proverb.

The early bird catches the worm.

someone who is energetic and efficient is most likely to be successful; English proverb, mid 17th century; compare **It's the second mouse that gets the cheese** below.

Preparation and Readiness

The early man never borrows from the late man.
someone who has made their preparations has no need to
turn to someone less efficient; English proverb, mid
17th century.

Forewarned is forearmed.
if one has been warned in advance about a problem one can
make preparations for dealing with it; English proverb, early
16th century.

**For want of a nail the shoe was lost; for want of a
shoe the horse was lost; and for want of a horse the
man was lost.**
often quoted allusively to imply that one apparently small
circumstance can result in a large-scale disaster; English
proverb, early 17th century (late 15th century in French).

Have an umbrella ready before it rains.
be sure you are prepared for difficult times; modern saying.

Hope for the best and prepare for the worst.
recommending a balance between optimism and realism;
English proverb, mid 16th century.

If you want peace, you must prepare for war.
a country in a state of military preparedness is unlikely to
be attacked; English proverb, mid 16th century; the idea is
found in the classical world in the *Nicomachaean Ethics* of
Aristotle, 'We make war that we may live in peace.'

Preparation and Readiness

It's the second mouse that gets the cheese.
modern addition to **The early bird catches the worm**
above, suggesting the dangers of being the first to make a
venture, and the possible benefits of following directly
behind a pioneer; compare **The only free cheese is in a
mousetrap** at TEMPTATION.

Measure seven times, cut once.
care taken in preparation will prevent errors (originally
referring to carpentry and needlework); Russian proverb.

No one was ever lost on a straight road.
if you know where you are going you will not make
mistakes; Indian proverb.

Pick your battles.
modern saying.

No plan survives first contact with the enemy.
modern saying, from the German soldier and statesman
Helmuth von Moltke (1800–91), 'No plan of operations
reaches with any certainly beyond the first encounter with
the enemy's main force.'

**Prayer to God, and service to the tsar, are
never wasted.**
Russian proverb.

To fail to prepare is to prepare to fail.
modern saying.

The Present

See also THE FUTURE, THE PAST

Although it may seem that what we want never arrives (Jam tomorrow and jam yesterday, but never jam today), *we should not lose sight of the fact that the present is what we have:* Yesterday has gone, tomorrow is yet to be. Today is the miracle.

Better an egg today than a hen tomorrow.

take advantage of what is available now, rather than waiting for possible advantages later; English proverb.

Enjoy the present moment and don't grieve for the future.

American proverb, mid 20th century.

Jam tomorrow and jam yesterday, but never jam today.

English proverb, late 19th century, from Lewis Carroll *Through the Looking-Glass* (1872), 'The rule is, jam to-morrow and jam yesterday—but never jam today!'

Yesterday has gone, tomorrow is yet to be. Today is the miracle.

modern saying.

Yesterday is ashes; tomorrow is wood. Only today does the fire burn brightly.

emphasizing the importance of enjoying and valuing the present rather than dwelling in the past, which cannot be changed, or the future, which has not yet happened; Canadian saying, said to be of Inuit origin.

Pride

See also SELF-ESTEEM AND SELF-ASSERTION

Pride may shield us from distress (Pride feels no pain), *but the shelter is not likely to last:* Pride goes before a fall.

He that will not stoop for a pin [a penny] will never be worth a point [a pound].

if pride prevents you from taking a small benefit, you will not make further gains; English proverb.

Pride feels no pain.

implying that inordinate self-esteem will not allow the admission that one might be suffering; English proverb, early 17th century.

Pride goes before a fall.

often with the implication that proud and haughty behaviour will contribute to its own downfall; English proverb, late 14th century, often with allusion to the Bible

(Proverbs 16:18), 'Pride goeth before destruction, and an haughty spirit before a fall.'

Stupidity and pride grow on the same tree.
pride is likely to blind us to a wise course of action; German proverb.

Problems and Solutions

See also WAYS AND MEANS

A particular situation or course of action is likely to affect what you then do: If you lead your mule to the top of the minaret, then you must lead him down again.

If you lead your mule to the top of the minaret, then you must lead him down again.
if you get yourself into a difficult position, you will have to extricate yourself; Arab proverb.

Never bid the Devil good morrow until you meet him.
a warning against trying to deal with problems or difficulties before they have actually occurred; English proverb, late 19th century, said to be an old Irish saying.

When all you have is a hammer, everything looks like a nail.

often used to comment on the wholesale application of one solution or method to the solution of any problem; English proverb, late 20th century (chiefly North America).

Why did the chicken cross the road?

traditional puzzle question, to which the answer is, 'to get to the other side'; mid 19th century.

Punctuality

See also TIME

Punctuality shows a proper courtesy (Punctuality is the politeness of princes), *and also has practical advantages:* First come, first served.

Better late than never.

even if one has missed the first chance of doing something, it is better to attempt it than not to do it at all; English proverb, early 14th century.

First come, first served.

English proverb, late 14th century.

Punctuality is the art of guessing correctly how late the other party is going to be.

American proverb, mid 20th century.

Punishment

Punctuality is the politeness of princes.
English proverb, mid 19th century; the idea is found earlier in French, in a comment by Louis XVIII (1755–1824), 'Punctuality is the politeness of kings.'

Punctuality is the soul of business.
English proverb, mid 19th century.

❈ Punishment

See CRIME AND PUNISHMENT

Quantities and Qualities

From Little fish are sweet *to* One spoonful of tar spoils a barrel of honey, *there is a consensus that a small quantity of something can be potent.*

All that glitters is not gold.

an attractive appearance is not necessarily evidence of intrinsic value; English proverb, early 13th century.

Drops that gather one by one finally become a sea.

Persian proverb.

How long is a piece of string?

traditional saying, used to indicate that something cannot be given a finite measurement.

Little fish are sweet.

small gifts are always acceptable; English proverb, early 19th century.

Many a little makes a mickle.

the proper form of the proverb **Many a mickle makes a muckle** below (*mickle* in Scottish usage means 'a large quantity or amount'); English proverb, mid 13th century.

Many a mickle makes a muckle.

an alteration of the proverb **Many a little makes a mickle** above; the result is actually nonsensical, since *muckle* is a variant of *mickle*, and both mean 'a large quantity or amount'.

The more the merrier.
English proverb, late 14th century.

The nearer the bone, the sweeter the meat.
the juiciest meat lies next to the bone, or the meat closest to the bone is particularly precious because it may represent one's last scrap of food; English proverb, late 14th century.

Never mind the quality, feel the width.
used as the title of a television comedy series (1967–9) about a tailoring business in the East End of London, ultimately probably an inversion of a cloth trade saying.

One spoonful of tar spoils a barrel of honey.
Russian proverb.

Small is beautiful.
title of a book by E. F. Schumacher, 1973.

There is safety in numbers.
now with the implication that a number of people will be unscathed where an individual might be in danger; English proverb, late 17th century.

Where's the beef?
advertising slogan for Wendy's Hamburgers in a campaign launched 9 January 1984, and subsequently taken up by the

American politician Walter Mondale in a televised debate with Gary Hart during the campaign for the US presidential campaign, 11 March 1984: 'When I hear your new ideas I'm reminded of that ad, "Where's the beef?" '

The whole is more than the sum of the parts.

traditional saying, probably deriving from Aristotle *Metaphysica*, 'Whenever anything which has several parts is such that the whole is something over and above its parts, and not just the sum of them, like a heap, then it always has some cause.'

You can count the apples on one tree, but not the trees in one apple.

African proverb.

Rank

The implicit acceptance of the desirability of social rank in It takes three generations to make a gentleman *is questioned by the traditional rhyme from the time of the Peasants' Revolt:* When Adam delved and Eve span, who was then the gentleman?

Everybody loves a lord.
English proverb, mid 19th century.

If two ride on a horse, one must ride behind.
of two people engaged on the same task, one must take a subordinate role; English proverb, late 16th century.

It takes three generations to make a gentleman.
English proverb, early 19th century; the idea that it took three generations before the possession of wealth conferred the status of gentleman occurs from the late 16th century.

When Adam delved and Eve span, who was then the gentleman?
traditional rhyme taken in this form by John Ball as the text of his revolutionary sermon on the outbreak of the Peasants' Revolt, 1381; it appears in the writings of Richard Rolle of Hampole (1290–1349) as, 'When Adam dalfe and Eve spane /Go spire if thou may spede, /Where was than the pride of man /That now merres his mede?'

Where Macgregor sits is the head of the table.

sometimes attributed to 'Rob Roy' MacGregor (other names
are used as well as Macgregor); English proverb, mid
19th century.

**You may know a gentleman by his horse, his hawk,
and his greyhound.**

traditional accoutrements of leisure for those of rank;
Welsh proverb.

Readiness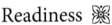

See PREPARATION AND READINESS

Reading

See also BOOKS

Reading is not only a valuable activity (The man who
reads is the man who leads), *it can provide a bond:* It
is a tie between men to have read the same book.

He that runs may read.

meaning very clear and readable; English proverb, late
16th century, originally with allusion to the Bible (Habakkuk
2:2), 'Write the vision, and make it plain upon tables, that
he may run that readeth it', reinforced by John Keble's
'Septuagesima' (1827), 'There is a book, who runs may read.'

Rebellion

It is a tie between men to have read the same book.
American proverb, mid 19th century.

The man who reads is the man who leads.
American proverb, mid 20th century.

 # Rebellion

See REVOLUTION AND REBELLION

 # Relationships

See also FEELINGS, FRIENDSHIP, LOVE

*Proverbial wisdom reflects both on relationships
between individuals* (There is always one who kisses,
and one who turns the cheek)*, and the wider link
between the individual and society* (I am because we
are; we are because I am).

I am because we are; we are because I am.
whatever affects the individual affects the whole community
and whatever affects the whole community affects the
individual; African proverb.

It is easy to kindle a fire on a familiar hearth.
a relationship which has once existed can be revived;
Welsh proverb.

L'amour est aveugle; l'amitié ferme les yeux.

French proverb, meaning that love is blind, while friendship closes its eyes; compare **Love is blind** at LOVE.

There is always one who kisses, and one who turns (or offers) the cheek.

traditional saying, said to be of French origin.

Treat a man as he is, and that is what he remains. Treat a man as he can be, and that is what he becomes.

modern saying, from Goethe *Wilhelm Meisters Lehrjare* (1795–6), 'When we take people, thou wouldst say, merely as they are, we make them worse; when we treat them as if they were what they should be, we improve them as far as they can be improved.'

Religion ✤

See also THE CHRISTIAN CHURCH, THE CLERGY, GOD

Religious practice is seen as a way of life: Laborare est orare [To work is to pray].

The family that prays together stays together.

motto devised by Al Scalpone for the Roman Catholic Family Rosary Crusade, 1947.

Reputation

Laborare est orare.

Latin, 'To work is to pray', a traditional motto of the
Benedictine order, also found in the form '*Ora, lege, et
labora* [Pray, read, and work].'

Man's extremity is God's opportunity.

great distress or danger may prompt a person to turn to
God for help; English proverb, early 17th century.

When you pray, move your feet.

advocating works as well as faith; saying, said to be of
Quaker origin.

※ Reputation

See also FAME

Not only is a good reputation a positive advantage
(When a tiger dies it leaves its skin. When a man dies
he leaves his name), *to acquire a bad reputation can be
dangerous, since there is ready belief in the idea that
there is* No smoke without fire.

De mortuis nil nisi bonum.

Latin, literally the injunction 'Of the dead, speak kindly or
not at all'; compare **Never speak ill of the dead** below.

The devil is not so black as he is painted.

someone may not be as bad as their reputation; English
proverb, mid 16th century.

A good name is better than a golden girdle.

French proverb.

A good reputation stands still; a bad one runs.

American proverb, mid 20th century.

He that has an ill name is half hanged.

someone with a bad reputation is already half way to being condemned on any charge brought against them; English proverb, late 14th century; compare **Give a dog a bad name and hang him** at GOSSIP.

A man's best reputation for his future is his record of the past.

American proverb, mid 20th century.

Never speak ill of the dead.

English proverb, mid 16th century; see *De mortuis nil nisi bonum* above.

No smoke without fire.

rumour is generally founded on fact; English proverb, late 14th century, earlier in French and Latin.

One may steal a horse, while another may not look over a hedge.

while one person is endlessly indulged, another is treated with suspicion on the slightest evidence; English proverb, mid 16th century.

Responsibility

Speak as you find.
English proverb, late 16th century.

Throw dirt enough, and some will stick.
persistent slander will in the end be believed; English
proverb, mid 17th century.

**When a tiger dies it leaves its skin. When a man dies
he leaves his name.**
a person leaves behind more than a body; Japanese proverb.

✼ Responsibility

*It is as well to be ready to take responsibility for
ourselves, since* Don't care was made to care; *however,
there is an awareness that there may be a price to be
paid:* Take what you want, and pay for it, says God.

Don't care was made to care.
traditional rebuke to someone who has asserted their lack of
concern; from the first words of a children's rhyme, 'Don't
care was made to care, don't care was hung'; English saying,
mid 20th century.

Everybody's business is nobody's business.
when something is of some interest to everyone, no single
person takes full responsibility for it; English proverb, early
17th century.

Every herring must hang by its own gill.

everyone is accountable for their own actions; English proverb, early 17th century.

Take what you want, and pay for it, says God.

traditional saying, sometimes said to be of Spanish origin.

Those who eat salty fish will have to accept being thirsty.

everyone is responsible for the consequences of their own actions; Chinese proverb.

Revenge ✺

It is tempting to seek revenge (Revenge is sweet), *but the unforgiving person may achieve more than they intend:* An eye for an eye makes the whole world blind.

Don't cut off your nose to spite your face.

warning against spiteful revenge which is likely to result in your own hurt or loss; English proverb, mid 16th century.

Don't get mad, get even.

late 20th-century saying.

An eye for an eye makes the whole world blind.

modern saying, often attributed to Mahatma Gandhi (1869–1948); often with allusion to the Bible (Exodus 21:23), 'Life for life, /Eye for eye, tooth for tooth.'

He laughs last who laughs best.
the most successful person is the one who is finally triumphant; English proverb, early 17th century.

He who laughs last, laughs longest.
early 20th-century saying.

If you want revenge, dig two graves.
pursuit of revenge is likely to be destructive to the pursuer as well as to their object; saying, claimed to be of Chinese or Japanese origin.

Living well is the best revenge.
traditional saying.

Revenge is a dish that can be eaten cold.
vengeance need not be exacted immediately; English proverb, late 19th century.

Revenge is sweet.
English proverb, mid 16th century.

Revolution and Rebellion

A revolution may begin with an idea (Every revolution was first a thought in one's man's mind), *but it will end in violence:* Revolutions are not made with rosewater.

Every revolution was first a thought in one man's mind.

American proverb, mid 19th century.

Revolutions are not made by men in spectacles.

American proverb, late 19th century.

Revolutions are not made with rosewater.

revolutions involve violence and ruthless behaviour; English proverb, early 19th century.

Whosoever draws his sword against the prince must throw away the scabbard.

anyone who tries to assassinate or depose a monarch must remain constantly on the defence; English proverb, early 17th century.

Rivers ❀

Rivers may have their own identity, but in the end they come to same place: All rivers run into the sea.

All rivers run into the sea.

English proverb, early 16th century; originally with allusion to the Bible (Ecclesiastes 1:7), 'All the rivers run into the sea; yet the sea is not full; unto the place from whence the rivers come, thither they return again.'

Royalty

Says Tweed to Till—'What gars ye rin sae still?' Says Till to Tweed—'Though ye rin with speed And I rin slaw, For ae man that ye droon I droon twa.'

traditional Scottish rhyme.

 Royalty

The royalty of a sovereign confers a special quality (The king can do no wrong)*, but in lesser figures may not be greatly regarded:* Camels, fleas, and princes exist everywhere.

Camels, fleas, and princes exist everywhere.

referring to the large numbers of offspring of some rulers; Persian proverb.

The king can do no wrong.

something cannot be wrong if it is done by someone of sovereign power, who alone is not subject to the law of the land; translation of the Latin legal maxim *rex non potest peccare*; English proverb, mid 17th century.

A king's chaff is worth more than other men's corn.

even minor benefits available to those attending on a sovereign are more substantial than the best that can be offered by those of lesser status; English proverb, early 17th century.

Satisfaction and Discontent

Satisfaction is most likely to be found by making the best of what is available: Half a loaf is better than no bread.

Acorns were good till bread was found.

until something better is found, what one has will be judged satisfactory; English proverb, late 16th century.

The answer is a lemon.

a *lemon* as the type of something unsatisfactory, perhaps referring to the least valuable symbol in a fruit machine; English proverb, early 20th century.

Better are small fish than an empty dish.

a little is preferable to nothing at all; English proverb, late 17th century.

Do not grieve that rose trees have thorns, rather rejoice that thorny bushes bear roses.

advocating an emphasis on positive aspects; Arab proverb; compare **No rose without a thorn** at CIRCUMSTANCE AND SITUATION, and **He who wants a rose must respect the thorn** at PRACTICALITY.

Go further and fare worse.

it is often wise to take what is on offer; English proverb, mid 16th century.

Sayings

Half a loaf is better than no bread.
to have part of something is better than having nothing at all; English proverb, mid 16th century.

Something is better than nothing.
even a possession of intrinsically little value is preferable to being empty-handed; English proverb, mid 16th century.

What you've never had you've never missed.
English proverb, early 20th century.

 # Sayings

See also WORDS

Common wisdom is often enshrined in popular sayings:
Proverbs are the coins of the people.

The devil can quote Scripture for his own ends.
it is possible for someone engaged in wrongdoing to quote selectively from the Bible in apparent support of their position, and alluding to the temptation of Christ by the Devil in the Bible (Matthew); English proverb, late 16th century.

Proverbs are the coins of the people.
Russian proverb.

There is no proverb without a grain of truth.
Russian proverb.

To understand the people acquaint yourself with their proverbs.

Arab proverb.

Traduttore traditore.

Italian, meaning 'Translators, traitors.'

Science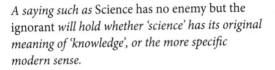

A saying such as Science has no enemy but the ignorant *will hold whether 'science' has its original meaning of 'knowledge', or the more specific modern sense.*

Laws of Thermodynamics:
1) You cannot win, you can only break even.
2) You can only break even at absolute zero.
3) You cannot reach absolute zero.

folklore among physicists.

Much science, much sorrow.

suggesting that learning may increase one's awareness of difficult questions; English proverb, early 17th century.

Science has no enemy but the ignorant.

English proverb, mid 16th century, from Latin *Scientia non habet inimicum nisi ignorantem.*

The Sea

Recommendations about seamanship are alive to the dangers of the sea: He that would go to sea for pleasure would go to hell for a pastime.

The good seaman is known in bad weather.
American proverb, mid 18th century.

He that would go to sea for pleasure would go to hell for a pastime.
with reference to the dangers involved in going to sea; English proverb, late 19th century.

If the Bermudas let you pass, you must beware of Hatteras.
traditional saying on the dangers of sailing in the Atlantic, and especially of the waters around Cape Hatteras in North Carolina.

One hand for oneself and one for the ship.
literally, hold on with one hand, and work the ship with the other; English proverb, late 18th century.

The sea wants to be visited.
referring to those who make their living from the sea; Scottish saying.

Secrecy

While it may be desirable to keep information confidential (Don't ask, don't tell, One does not wash one's dirty linen in public)*, it is likely to be difficult:* Fields have eyes and woods have ears.

The day has eyes, the night has ears.

there is always someone watching or listening; traditional saying.

Dead men tell no tales.

often used to imply that a person's knowledge of a secret will die with them; English proverb, mid 17th century.

Don't ask, don't tell.

summary of the Clinton administration's compromise policy on homosexuals serving in the armed forces, as described by Sam Nunn (1938–) in May 1993.

Fields have eyes and woods have ears.

one may always be spied on by unseen watchers or listeners; English proverb, early 13th century.

Listeners never hear good of themselves.

English proverb, mid 17th century.

Little pitchers have large ears.

children overhear what is not meant for them (a pitcher's *ears* are its handles); English proverb, mid 16th century.

Secrecy

Never tell tales out of school.
a warning against indiscretion; English proverb, mid 16th century.

No names, no pack drill.
if nobody is named as being responsible, nobody can be blamed or punished (*pack drill* = a military punishment of walking up and down carrying full equipment); English proverb, early 20th century; the expression is now used generally to express an unwillingness to provide detailed information.

One does not wash one's dirty linen in public.
discreditable matters should be dealt with privately; English proverb, early 19th century.

A secret is either too good to keep or too bad not to tell.
American proverb, mid 20th century.

See all your best work go unnoticed.
advertisement for staff for MI5, 2005.

Those who hide can find.
those who have concealed something know where it is to be found; English proverb, early 15th century.

Three may keep a secret, if two of them are dead.
the only way to keep a secret is to tell no one else; English proverb, mid 16th century.

Walls have ears.

care should be taken for possible eavesdroppers; English proverb, late 16th century.

What is done by night appears by day.

secrets are likely to be revealed; English proverb.

Will the real — please stand up?

catchphrase from an American TV game show (1955–66) in which a panel was asked to identify the 'real' one of three candidates all claiming to be a particular person; after the guesses were made, the compère would request the 'real' candidate to stand up.

You can't hide an awl in a sack.

some things are too conspicuous to hide; Russian proverb.

Self-Esteem and Self-Assertion

See also PRIDE

A saying such as The bigger the hat, the smaller the property *suggests self-assertion, but more traditional sayings warn against boasting of one's attributes:* Clever hawks conceal their claws.

The bigger the hat, the smaller the property.

Australian saying.

Self-Esteem and Self-Assertion

Clever hawks conceal their claws.
it is not necessary to boast of one's abilities;
Japanese proverb.

Deny self for self's sake.
the result of self-denial is likely to be self-improvement;
American proverb, mid 18th century.

A frog in a well knows nothing of the ocean.
one should be aware of the limitations of one's own
experience; Japanese proverb.

Here's tae us; wha's like us?
Gey few, and they're a' deid.
Scottish toast, probably of 19th century origin.

Know thyself.
English proverb, late 14th century; inscribed in Greek on
the temple of Apollo at Delphi; Plato, in *Protagoras,* ascribes
the saying to the Seven Wise Men of the 6th century BC.

The kumara does not speak of its own sweetness.
one should not praise oneself (a *kumara* is a sweet potato);
Maori proverb.

**The peacock is always happy because it never looks
at its ugly feet.**
a person does not see their own faults; Persian proverb.

Self-praise is no recommendation.

a person's own favourable account of themselves is of
dubious worth; English proverb, early 19th century.

Self-Interest

Pragmatic advice on watching your own interests
(Self-preservation is the first law of nature) *may be set
against reflections on fulfilling one's one responsibilities:*
If every man would sweep his own doorstep the city
would soon be clean.

Every man for himself and God for us all.

ultimately God is concerned for humankind while
individuals are concerned only for themselves; English
proverb, mid 16th century.

Every man for himself, and the Devil take the hindmost.

each person must look out for their own interests, and the
weakest is likely to come to disaster; English proverb, early
16th century.

Every man is the architect of his own fortune.

each person is ultimately responsible for what happens to
them; English proverb, mid 16th century.

Self-Interest

Hear all, see all, say nowt, tak' all, keep all, gie nowt, and if tha ever does owt for nowt do it for thysen.

now associated with Yorkshire, and caricaturing supposedly traditional Yorkshire attributes, in the picture of someone who is shrewd, taciturn, grasping, and selfish; English proverb, early 15th century.

If every man would sweep his own doorstep the city would soon be clean.

if everyone fulfils their own responsibilities, what is necessary will be done; English proverb, early 17th century.

If you want a thing done well, do it yourself.

no one else has so much interest in your own welfare; English proverb, mid 17th century.

If you would be well served, serve yourself.

no one else has so much interest in your own welfare; English proverb, mid 17th century.

Near is my kirtle, but nearer my smock.

used as a justification for putting one's own interests first (a *kirtle* is a woman's skirt or gown, and a *smock* is an undergarment); English proverb, mid 15th century.

Near is my shirt, but nearer my skin.

a justification of self-interest; English proverb, late 16th century.

A satisfied person does not know the hungry person.

African proverb.

Self-interest is the rule, self-sacrifice the exception.

American proverb, mid 20th century.

Self-preservation is the first law of nature.

the instinct for self-preservation is inbuilt and instinctive;
English proverb, mid 17th century.

Selling

See BUYING AND SELLING

Sex

See also LOVE, MARRIAGE

A question such as Did the earth move for you?
*suggests a less bleak view of sex than the dismissive
view that* Dirty water will quench fire.

Did the earth move for you?

supposedly said to one's partner after sexual intercourse,
after Ernest Hemingway *For Whom the Bell Tolls* (1940),
'But did thee feel the earth move.'

Sickness

Dirty water will quench fire.

mainly used to mean that a man's sexual needs can be satisfied by any woman, however ugly or immoral; English proverb, mid 16th century.

Post coitum omne animal triste.

Latin, 'After coition every animal is sad.'

Why buy a cow when milk is so cheap?

putting forward an argument for choosing the least troublesome alternative; frequently used as an argument against marriage; English proverb, mid 17th century.

✵ Sickness

See also HEALTH, MEDICINE

While sickness should be avoided, ailments are not necessarily fatal: A creaking door hangs longest.

Coughs and sneezes spread diseases. Trap the germs in your handkerchief.

Second World War health slogan (1942).

A creaking door hangs longest.

someone who is apparently in poor health may well outlive the ostensibly stronger; English proverb, late 17th century.

Diseases come on horseback but go away on foot.

sickness may occur swiftly, but recovery is likely to be slow; English proverb, late 16th century.

Feed a cold and starve a fever.

probably intended as two separate admonitions, but
sometimes interpreted to mean that if you feed a cold you will
have to starve a fever later; English proverb, mid 19th century.

From the bitterness of disease, man learns the sweetness of health.

Catalan proverb.

An imaginary ailment is worse than a disease.

Yiddish proverb.

Silence

See also SPEECH

Silence can be impressive in itself (Silence is a still
noise) *as well as a guard against idle talk:* A shut
mouth catches no flies.

A shut mouth catches no flies.

a warning against the dangers of idle talk; English proverb,
late 16th century.

Silence is a still noise.

American proverb, late 19th century.

Silence means consent.

English proverb, late 14th century; translation of a Latin tag,
'*Qui tacet consentire videtur* [He who is silent seems to

consent]', said to have been spoken by Thomas More (1478–1535) when asked at his trial why he was silent on being asked to acknowledge the king's supremacy over the Church. The principle is not accepted in modern English law.

Speech is silver, but silence is golden.

discretion can be more valuable than the most eloquent words; English proverb, mid 19th century; compare **Who knows most, speaks least** at SPEECH.

Speech sows, silence reaps.

once an argument has been put, it is wise to give time for the words to have an effect; saying, said to be a Persian proverb.

A still tongue makes a wise head.

a person who is not given to idle talk, and who listens to others, is likely to be wise; English proverb, mid 16th century.

※ Similarity and Difference

Similarity may be a bond (Birds of a feather flock together), *or may promote rivalry:* Two swords cannot fit in one scabbard.

All cats are grey in the dark.

darkness obscures inessential differences; English proverb, mid 16th century.

Similarity and Difference

Birds of a feather flock together.

people of the same (usually unscrupulous) character tend to associate; English proverb, mid 16th century.

Comparisons are odious.

often used to suggest that to compare two different things or persons is unhelpful or misleading; English proverb, mid 15th century.

East is east, and west is west.

an assertion of ineradicable racial and cultural differences; English proverb, late 19th century, from Kipling 'The Ballad of East and West' (1892), 'Oh, East is East, and West is West, and never the twain shall meet, Till Earth and Sky stand presently at God's great Judgement Seat; But there is neither East nor West, Border, nor Breed, nor Birth, When two strong men stand face to face, tho' they come from the ends of the earth!'

Extremes meet.

opposite extremes have much in common; English proverb, mid 18th century.

From the sweetest wine, the tartest vinegar.

the strongest hate comes from former love; English proverb, late 16th century.

Like breeds like.

a particular kind of event may well be the genesis of a similar occurrence; English proverb, mid 16th century.

Situation

Like will to like.

those of similar nature and inclination are drawn together;
English proverb, late 14th century.

One nail drives out another.

like will counter like; English proverb, mid 13th century.

Two of a trade never agree.

close association with someone makes disagreement over policy
and principles more likely; English proverb, early 17th century.

Two swords do not fit in one scabbard.

Indian proverb.

When Greek meets Greek, then comes the tug of war.

when two people of a similar kind are opposed, there is a
struggle for supremacy; English proverb, late 17th century,
from Nathaniel Lee *The Rival Queens* (1677), 'When Greeks
joined Greeks, then was the tug of war!'

 # Situation

See CIRCUMSTANCE AND SITUATION

 # Sleep

See also DREAMS

Sleep is a source of essential refreshment (One hour's
sleep before midnight is worth two after), *but*

overindulgence in it is a bad sign: Some sleep five
hours; nature requires seven, laziness nine, and
wickedness eleven.

The beginning of health is sleep.
Irish proverb.

The morning knows more than the evening.
the mind is clearer after sleep; Russian proverb.

**One hour's sleep before midnight is worth
two after.**
English proverb, mid 17th century.

**Six hours' sleep for a man, seven for a woman, and
eight for a fool.**
implying that the more sleep a person needs, the less
vigorous and effective they are likely to be; English proverb,
early 17th century.

**Some sleep five hours; nature requires seven,
laziness nine, and wickedness eleven.**
American proverb, mid 20th century.

We never sleep.
motto of the American detective agency founded by Allan
Pinkerton (*c.*1855).

Smoking

Sayings about smoking trace a changing attitude to the habit, culminating in the warning Smoking can seriously damage your health.

Coffee without tobacco is like a Jew without a rabbi.
Moroccan proverb.

Happiness is a cigar called Hamlet.
advertising slogan for Hamlet cigars, UK.

More doctors recommend Camels than any other cigarette.
advertising slogan for Camel cigarettes.

Smoking can seriously damage your health.
government health warning now required by British law to be printed on cigarette packets; in the form 'Smoking can damage your health' from early 1970s.

You're never alone with a Strand.
advertising slogan for Strand cigarettes, 1960; the image of loneliness was so strongly conveyed by the solitary smoker that sales were adversely affected.

Solitude

While you may be hampered by companionship (He travels the fastest who travels alone), *there are risks in solitude:* The lone sheep is in danger of the wolf.

Better alone than in bad company.
American proverb, late 17th century.

He travels the fastest who travels alone.
implying that single-minded pursuit of an objective is more easily achieved by someone without family commitments; English proverb, late 19th century; from Kipling 'The Winners' (1890), 'Down to Gehenna or up to the Throne, He travels the fastest who travels alone.'

The lone sheep is in danger of the wolf.
stressing the importance of mutual support; English proverb, late 16th century.

No man is an island.
every person has some connection with and responsibility for others; saying from John Donne's 'Meditation XVII' from 'Devotions upon Emergent Occasions' (1624).

Solutions

See PROBLEMS AND SOLUTIONS

Sorrow

See also MOURNING, SUFFERING

Grief is inevitable, but we may find ways of dealing with it—perhaps by seeking the support of others: Misery loves company.

He that conceals his grief, finds no remedy for it.

trying to hide distress means that you do not recover from it; proverb, said to be of Turkish origin.

Misery loves company.

English proverb, late 16th century, now predominantly current in the United States.

Wednesday's child is full of woe.

traditional rhyme, mid 19th century (compare qualities associated with birth on other days at entries under BEAUTY, GIFTS, TRAVEL, and WORK).

You cannot prevent the birds of sorrow from flying overhead, but you can prevent them from building nests in your hair.

sorrow may be unavoidable, but one can respond to it in different ways; Chinese proverb.

Speech

While conversation is endorsed by the slogan It's good to talk, *there is a traditional consensus that concision in speech is desirable:* Length begets loathing.

Brevity is the soul of wit.

English proverb, early 17th century, from Shakespeare *Henry IV, Part 2* (1597).

If I listen, I have the advantage; if I speak, others have it.

a warning against rushing into speech; Arabic proverb.

It's good to talk.

advertising slogan for British Telecom from 1994.

Length begets loathing.

in reference to verbosity; English proverb, mid 18th century.

Listen a thousand times, and speak once.

warning against making a hasty response; Turkish proverb.

Who knows most, speaks least.

English proverb, mid 17th century.

Sports and Games

The saying Nice guys finish last *might be applied to the results of a number of games.*

Spring

Chess is a sea where a gnat may drink and an elephant may bathe.

the game may be played at many levels; modern saying, said to derive from an Indian proverb.

Drive for show, and putt for dough.

Golf saying meaning that matches are won in the final strokes on the green, and not by the opening drive from the tee.

Nice guys finish last.

modern saying, from a casual remark by the American coach Leo Durocher (1906–91), 'I called off his players' names as they came marching up the steps behind him...All nice guys. They'll finish last. Nice guys. Finish last.'

Spring

See also AUTUMN, SUMMER, WINTER

Individual months have their own character (March comes in like a lion, and goes out like a lamb), *but spring as a season depends on progression:* April showers bring forth May flowers.

April and May are the keys to the whole year.

good weather in April and May lays an essential foundation for the rest of the year; German proverb.

April showers bring forth May flowers.

English proverb.

A cold April the barn will fill.

cold weather in April is likely to mean a good harvest later in the year; traditional saying.

A cold May and windy, a full barn will find ye.

Cold and windy weather in May is a predictor of a good harvest; traditional saying; in its original form, 'a full barn and findy [an obsolete word meaning "weighty, plentiful"]'.

March borrowed from April three days, and they were ill.

English proverb.

March comes in like a lion, and goes out like a lamb.

English proverb.

May chickens come cheeping.

English proverb.

On the first of March, the crows begin to search.

English proverb.

A peck of March dust is worth a king's ransom.

English proverb.

Rain in spring is as precious as oil.

Chinese proverb.

Strength and Weakness

So many mists in March, so many frosts in May.
English proverb.

Spring is sooner recognized by plants than by men.
Chinese proverb.

✵ Strength and Weakness

Individuals may be specially gifted with strength (Only an elephant can bear an elephant's load), *but there may be an interrelationship between the strong and the weak:* The caribou feeds the wolf, but it is the wolf that keeps the caribou strong.

The caribou feeds the wolf, but it is the wolf that keeps the caribou strong.
stressing the interrelationship between predator and prey; Inuit proverb.

An elephant does not die of one broken rib.
a strong person will not be brought down by a minor injury; African proverb.

Every tub must stand on its own bottom.
it is necessary to support oneself by one's own efforts; English proverb, mid 16th century.

If you are afraid of wolves, don't go into the forest.
Russian proverb.

Strength and Weakness

If you don't like the heat, get out of the kitchen.
if you choose to work in a particular sphere you must also
deal with its pressures; English proverb, mid 20th century,
from a comment associated with the American statesman
Harry S. Truman (though attributed by him to his 'military
jester' Harry Vaughan, 1893–1981), 'If you can't stand the
heat, get out of the kitchen.'

It is the pace that kills.
used as a warning against working under extreme pressure;
English proverb, mid 19th century.

Only an elephant can bear an elephant's load.
heavy responsibilities require significant strength; Indian
proverb (Marathi).

Only the eagle can gaze at the sun.
only a strong person can undertake a demanding task;
English proverb; late 16th century.

**A reed before the wind lives on, while mighty
oaks fall.**
something which bends to the force of the wind is less likely
to be broken than something which tries to withstand it;
English proverb, late 14th century.

Strength through joy.
German Labour Front slogan from 1933, coined by Robert
Ley (1890–1945).

Success and Failure

The weakest go to the wall.

usually said to derive from the installation of seating
(around the walls) in the churches of the late Middle Ages;
English proverb, early 16th century.

What does not kill you makes you stronger.

an encouragement in difficult circumstances;
modern saying.

You are the weakest link . . . goodbye.

catchphrase used by Anne Robinson on the television game
show *The Weakest Link* (2000–); compare **A chain is no
stronger than its weakest link** at COOPERATION.

✲ Success and Failure

See also WINNING AND LOSING

Success and failure are both part of life (You win a few,
you lose a few), *and it is wise to remember that notable
and sudden success is likely to be transient:* Up like a
rocket, down like a stick.

The bigger they are, the harder they fall.

English proverb, early 20th century, commonly attributed in
its current form to the boxer Robert Fitzsimmons, prior to a
fight, *c.*1900.

Do not laugh at the fallen; there may be slippery places ahead.

it is wise to remember when seeing someone in trouble that you too may have difficulties; African proverb.

From clogs to clogs is only three generations.

the *clog*, a shoe with a thick wooden sole, was worn by manual workers in the north of England. The implication is that the energy and ability required to raise a person's material status from poverty is often not continued to the third generation, and that the success is therefore not sustained; English proverb, late 19th century, said to be a Lancashire proverb.

From shirtsleeves to shirtsleeves in three generations.

wealth gained in one generation will be lost by the third; English proverb, early 20th century. The saying is often attributed to the Scottish-born American industrialist and philanthropist Andrew Carnegie (1835–1919) but is not found in his writings.

From the sublime to the ridiculous is only one step.

English proverb, late 19th century; the idea is found earlier in the writings of Thomas Paine *The Age of Reason* pt 2 (1795), 'The sublime and the ridiculous are often so nearly related, that it is difficult to class them separately. One step above the sublime, makes the ridiculous; and one step above the ridiculous, makes the sublime again.' A similar

Success and Failure

comment is found in a comment of Napoleon's after the 1812 retreat from Moscow, 'There is only one step from the sublime to the ridiculous.'

He who fails to plan, plans to fail.
modern saying.

He who leaves succeeds.
moving away from home territory leads to success; Italian proverb.

Let them laugh that win.
triumphant laughter should be withheld until success is assured; English proverb, mid 16th century.

Nothing succeeds like success.
someone already regarded as successful is likely to attract more support; English proverb, mid 19th century.

The only place where success comes before work is in a dictionary.
modern saying.

The race is not to the swift, nor the battle to the strong.
the person with the most apparent advantages will not necessarily be successful; English proverb, mid 17th century; often with allusion to the Bible (Ecclesiastes 9:11).

Success and Failure

A rising tide lifts all boats.

usually taken to mean that a prosperous society benefits
everybody; in America the expression was particularly
associated with John Fitzgerald Kennedy (1917–63); English
proverb, mid 20th century.

Rooster today, feather duster tomorrow.

one who is currently successful may subsequently find that
circumstances change dramatically; Australian saying.

Success has many fathers, while failure is an orphan.

once something is seen to succeed many people will claim
to have initiated it, while responsibility for failure is likely to
be disclaimed; English proverb, mid 20th century; the idea
is found in the diary (for 9 September 1942) of Mussolini's
son-in-law Count Galeazzo Ciano (1903–44), 'Victory has
a hundred fathers, but no one wants to recognise defeat
as his own.'

Up like a rocket, down like a stick.

sudden marked success is likely to be followed by equally
sudden failure; English proverb, late 19th century; the
simile is found earlier in Thomas Paine's (1737–1809)
comment on Edmund Burke's losing the parliamentary
debate on the French Revolution to Charles James Fox, 'As
he rose like a rocket, he fell like the stick.'

Suffering

When an elephant is in trouble, even a frog can kick him.

the weak can attack the strong when they are in difficulty; Indian proverb.

You win a few, you lose a few.

one has to accept failure as well as success, and used as an expression of consolation or resignation; English proverb, mid 20th century.

 # Suffering

See also MOURNING, SORROW, SYMPATHY

Suffering may ennoble (Crosses are ladders that lead to heaven)*, but the slogan* Beauty without cruelty *reminds us that we have no right to inflict it to satisfy our own wants.*

Beauty without cruelty.

slogan for Animal Rights.

Crosses are ladders that lead to heaven.

the way to heaven is through suffering; crosses refers either to the crucifix, or more generally to troubles or misfortunes; English proverb, early 17th century.

No cross, no crown.

cross is here used punningly, as in **Crosses are ladders that lead to heaven** above; English proverb, early 17th century.

Summer

See also AUTUMN, SPRING, WINTER

Summer may see the longest days of the year (Barnaby bright, Barnaby bright, the longest day and the shortest night), *but it does not necessarily imply good weather:* A dripping June sets all in tune.

Barnaby bright, Barnaby bright, the longest day and the shortest night.

in the Old Style calendar St Barnabas' Day, 11 June, was reckoned the longest day of the year; English proverb, mid 17th century.

A cherry year, a merry year; a plum year, a dumb year.

recording the tradition that a good crop of cherries is a promising sign for the year; English proverb, late 17th century.

A dripping June sets all in tune.

English proverb.

One swallow does not make a summer.

English proverb.

Surprise

Saint Swithin's day, if thou be fair, for forty days it will remain; Saint Swithin's day, if thou bring rain, for forty days it will remain.

Saint Swithin's day is 15 July, and the tradition may have its origin in the heavy rain said to have occurred when his relics were to be transferred to a shrine in Winchester Cathedral; English proverb, early 17th century.

Summer is the mother of the poor.

for someone living in poverty, summer is easier than cold weather; Italian proverb.

A swarm in May is worth a load of hay; a swarm in June is worth a silver spoon; but a swarm in July is not worth a fly.

traditional beekeepers' saying, meaning that the later in the summer it is, the less time there will be for bees to collect pollen from flowers in blossom; English proverb, mid 17th century.

✳ Surprise

A saying such as You could have knocked me down with a feather *suggests a lack of awareness that* The unexpected always happens.

The age of miracles is past.

often used ironically, or as a comment on failure; English proverb, late 16th century.

Nobody expects the Spanish Inquisition.

from the script of an episode of *Monty Python's Flying Circus* (BBC TV programme, 1970), 'Nobody expects the Spanish Inquisition! Our chief weapon is surprise—surprise and fear…fear and surprise…our two weapons are fear and surprise—and ruthless efficiency.…'

The unexpected always happens.

warning against an overconfident belief that something cannot occur; English proverb, late 19th century.

Wonders will never cease.

often used ironically to comment on an unusual circumstance; English proverb, late 18th century.

You could have knocked me down with a feather.

expressing great surprise; English saying, mid 19th century.

Sympathy

While we cannot necessarily depend on unstinting sympathy (Laugh and the world laughs with you, weep and you weep alone)*, to seek for it is natural:* One kind word warms three winter months.

God makes the back to the burden.

an assertion that nothing is truly insupportable used in resignation or consolation; English proverb, early 19th century.

Sympathy

God tempers the wind to the shorn lamb.
God so arranges it that bad luck does not unduly plague the weak or unfortunate; English proverb, mid 17th century.

Laugh and the world laughs with you, weep and you weep alone.
English proverb, late 19th century; in this form from the poem 'Solitude' by the American poet Ella Wheeler Wilcox (1855–1919), 'Laugh and the world laughs with you; Weep, and you weep alone'; ultimately echoing the Bible (Romans 16:15), 'Rejoice with them that do rejoice, and weep with them that weep', and Horace (c.65–8) *Ars Poetica,* 'Men's faces laugh on those who laugh, and correspondingly weep on those who weep.'

Nothing so bad but it might have been worse.
used in resignation or consolation; English proverb, late 19th century.

One kind word warms three winter months.
Japanese proverb.

Pity is akin to love.
English proverb, early 17th century.

The rock in the water does not know the pain of the rock in the sun.
awareness of your own suffering prevents you from understanding the pain of those in different circumstances; Hawaiian proverb.

Shared joy is double joy, and shared sorrow is double sorrow.

proverb, said to be of German origin.

The tears of the stranger are only water.

sympathy for grief may be limited to those whom we already know; Russian proverb.

Teaching

See also EDUCATION

Teaching is important (Who teaches me for a day is my father for a lifetime), *but it may have its limitations:* Tell me and I'll forget. Show me and I'll remember. Involve me and I'll be changed forever.

He teaches ill who teaches all.
English proverb, early 17th century.

He that teaches himself has a fool for a master.
English proverb, early 17th century.

Nobody forgets a good teacher.
Teacher Training Agency slogan, late 20th century.

Tell me and I'll forget. Show me and I'll remember. Involve me and I'll be changed forever.
Japanese proverb.

Who teaches me for a day is my father for a lifetime.
Chinese proverb; compare **Give a man a fish, and you feed him for a day; show him how to catch fish, and you feed him for a lifetime** at CHARITY.

Technology

See also CHANGE, COMPUTING, SCIENCE

Technology may provide us with solutions (You press the button, we do the rest)*, but it can also constrict us:* Science finds, industry applies, man conforms.

The camera never lies.
20th-century saying.

Let your fingers do the walking.
1960s advertisement for the Bell System Telephone Directory Yellow Pages.

Science finds, industry applies, man conforms.
subtitle of guidebook to 1933 Chicago World's Fair.

Vorsprung durch Technik.
German, 'Progress through technology', advertising slogan for Audi motors, from 1986.

You press the button, we do the rest.
advertising slogan to launch the Kodak camera 1888, coined by George Eastman (1854–1932).

Temptation

What is forbidden is particularly attractive (Naughty but nice); *however, the attraction is likely to conceal danger:* The only free cheese is in a mousetrap.

The bleating of the lamb excites the tiger.

of a prey staked out to attract a predator; Indian proverb; used by Kipling in *Stalky & Co.* (1899) in the form 'the bleating of the kid...'

Fish follow the bait.

English proverb, 17th century.

The fish will soon be caught that nibbles at every bait.

English proverb, 16th century.

Naughty but nice.

advertising slogan for cream cakes in the first half of the 1980s; earlier, the title of a 1939 film.

The only free cheese is in a mousetrap.

Russian proverb; compare **It's the second mouse that gets the cheese** at PREPARATION AND READINESS.

Stolen fruit are sweet.

The knowledge that something is forbidden makes it more attractive; English proverb, early 17th century.

Stolen waters are sweet.

something which has been obtained secretly or illicitly
seems particularly attractive; English proverb, late
14th century.

There's no such thing as a free lunch.

colloquial axiom in American economics from the mid
20th century, much associated with the economist Milton
Friedman (1912–2006), but not coined by him.

Thinking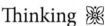

See also HYPOTHESIS AND FACT, OPINION

*Thought may or may not be original (Great minds
think alike), but we should exercise the faculty:* To
question and ask is a moment's shame, but to
question and not ask is a lifetime's shame.

Elementary, my dear Watson.

remark attributed to Sherlock Holmes, but not found in
this form in any book by Arthur Conan Doyle; first found
in P. G. Wodehouse *Psmith Journalist* (1915).

Great minds think alike.

English proverb, early 17th century, now often
used ironically.

Thoroughness

To question and ask is a moment's shame, but to question and not ask is a lifetime's shame.
Japanese proverb.

Two heads are better than one.
it is advisable to discuss a problem with another person; English proverb, late 14th century.

 # Thoroughness

See also DETERMINATION

Even if you are putting yourself at risk, thoroughness is to be recommended: Might as well be hanged for a sheep as for a lamb.

Do not spoil the ship for a ha'porth of tar.
used generally to warn against risking loss or failure through unwillingness to allow relatively trivial expenditure; *ship* is a dialectal pronunciation of *sheep,* and the original literal sense was 'do not allow sheep to die for the lack of a trifling amount of tar', *tar* being used to protect sores and wounds on sheep from flies; English proverb, early 17th century.

In for a penny, in for a pound.
If one is to be involved at all, it may as well be fully; English proverb, late 17th century.

Nothing venture, nothing gain.
a later variant of **Nothing venture, nothing have** below;
English proverb, early 17th century.

Nothing venture, nothing have.
one must be prepared to take some risks to gain a desired
end; English proverb, late 14th century.

One might as well be hanged for a sheep as a lamb.
if one is going to incur a severe penalty it may as well be for
something substantial; English proverb, late 17th century.

Thrift and Extravagance ✵

See also DEBT AND BORROWING, MONEY, POVERTY, WEALTH

*Thrift is not only desirable itself, but is likely to be
rewarded* (A penny saved is a penny earned)*; however,
it may be easier to admire than to practise it:* Most
people consider thrift a fine virtue in ancestors.

Bang goes sixpence.
ironic commentary on regretted expenditure, deriving from
a cartoon in *Punch* of 5 December 1868, featuring a miserly
Scotsman. The caption read, 'a had na' been the-erre abune
Twa Hoours when—Bang—went Saxpence!'

Make do and mend.
wartime slogan, 1940s.

Thrift and Extravagance

Most people consider thrift a fine virtue in ancestors.

American proverb, mid 20th century.

A penny saved is a penny earned.

used as an exhortation to thrift; English proverb, mid
17th century.

Penny wise and pound foolish.

too much concern with saving small sums may result in
larger loss if necessary expenditure on maintenance and
safety has been withheld; English proverb, early 17th century.

Spare at the spigot, and let out the bunghole.

referring to the practice of being overcareful on the one
hand, and carelessly generous on the other. A *spigot* is a peg
or pin used to regulate the flow of liquid through a tap on a
cask, and a *bunghole* is a hole through which a cask is filled
or emptied, and which is closed by a bung; English proverb,
mid 17th century.

Spare well and have to spend.

the person who is thrifty and careful with their resources
can use them lavishly when the occasion offers; English
proverb, mid 16th century.

**Stretch your arm no further than your sleeve
will reach.**

you should not spend more than you can afford; English
proverb, mid 16th century.

Take care of the pence and the pounds will take care of themselves.
thrift and small savings will grow to substantial wealth; English proverb, mid 18th century.

Thrift is a great revenue.
care with expenditure is one of the best ways of providing an income for oneself; English proverb, mid 17th century.

Wilful waste makes woeful want.
deliberate misuse of resources is likely to lead to severe shortage; English proverb, early 18th century.

Time

See also TRANSIENCE

Time is seen not only as a powerful force (Time works wonders), *but as one which is beyond any control:* An inch of gold cannot buy time.

Be the day weary or be the day long, at last it ringeth to evensong.
even the most difficult time will come to an end; English proverb, early 16th century.

Even a stopped clock is right twice a day.
modern humorous saying.

Time

An inch of gold cannot buy time.
time cannot be bought with money; Chinese proverb.

Man fears Time, but Time fears the Pyramids.
Egyptian proverb.

The morning daylight appears plainer when you put out your candle.
American proverb.

Never is a long time.
often used to indicate that circumstances may ultimately change; English proverb, late 14th century.

Spring forward, fall back.
a reminder that clocks are moved *forward* in the spring, and *back* in the fall (autumn).

There is a time for everything.
there is always a suitable time to do something; English proverb, late 14th century, from the Bible (Ecclesiastes 3:1), 'To every thing there is a season, and a time to every purpose under heaven.'

Time is a great healer.
initial pain is felt less keenly with the passage of time; English proverb, late 14th century.

Time will tell.

the true nature of something is likely to emerge over a period of time, and conversely it is only after time has passed that something can be regarded as settled; English proverb, mid 16th century.

Time works wonders.

often used to suggest that with the passage of time something initially unknown and unwelcome will become familiar and acceptable; English proverb, late 16th century.

You have the watches, but we have the time.

early 21st-century saying, said to be an Afghan saying addressed to ISAF/NATO forces.

Tolerance ※

See PREJUDICE AND TOLERANCE

Town ※

See THE COUNTRY AND THE TOWN

Towns and Cities ※

See also BRITISH TOWNS AND REGIONS

Individual cities may be seen as a spiritual as well as geographical centre: All roads lead to Rome.

Transience

All roads lead to Rome.
English proverb, late 14th century, earlier in Latin.

From Madrid to heaven, and in heaven a little window from which to look down on Madrid.
Spanish saying.

Isfahan is half the world.
Isfahan was the capital of Persia from 1598 until 1722; Persian proverb.

Next year in Jerusalem!
traditionally the concluding words of the Jewish Passover service, expressing the hope of the Diaspora that Jews dispersed throughout the world would once more be reunited.

See Naples and die.
implying that after seeing Naples, one could have nothing left on earth to wish for; Goethe noted it as an Italian proverb in his diary in 1787.

✸ Transience

See also OPPORTUNITY, TIME

Awareness of transience may be used as a comfort (And this, too, shall pass away) *or as a warning: Sic transit gloria mundi.*

And this, too, shall pass away.

traditional saying said to be true for all times and situations;
the story is told by Edward Fitzgerald in *Polonius* (1852),
'The Sultan asked for a signet motto, that should hold good
for Adversity or Prosperity, Solomon gave him—"This also
shall pass away."'

Sic transit gloria mundi.

Latin, 'Thus passes the glory of the world', said during the
coronation of a new Pope, while flax is burned (used at the
coronation of Alexander V in Pisa, 7 July 1409, but earlier
in origin).

Time flies.

English proverb, late 14th century, from Virgil (70–19 BC)
Georgics, 'Sedfugit interea, fugit inreparabile tempus [But
meanwhile it is flying, irretrievable time is flying].'

Travel ✽

See also COUNTRIES AND PEOPLES

Travel may provide us with many different experiences
(Every two miles the water changes, every twelve
miles the speech), *but we are also warned:* Go abroad
and you'll hear news of home.

Travel

Been there, done that, got the T-shirt.
evoking a jaded tourist as the image of someone who is bored by too much sightseeing.

Clunk, click, every trip.
road safety campaign promoting the use of seatbelts, 1971.

Every two miles the water changes, every twelve miles the speech.
commenting on the changes experienced by travellers (the number of miles varies); Indian proverb.

Go abroad and you'll hear news of home.
information about one's imnmediate vicinity may have become more widely publicized; English proverb, late 17th century.

Have gun, will travel.
supposedly characteristic statement of a hired gunman in a western; popularized as the title of an American television series (1957–64).

The heaviest baggage for the traveller is an empty purse.
travelling is difficult without the money to pay for it; German proverb.

If it's Tuesday, this must be Belgium.
late 20th-century saying, from the title of a 1969 film written by David Shaw.

If you don't know where you are going, any road will do.

modern saying, originally with allusion to Lewis Carroll.

Is your journey really necessary?

1939 slogan, coined to discourage Civil Servants from going home for Christmas.

Let the train take the strain.

British Rail slogan, 1970 onwards.

Roads are made by walking.

Spanish proverb.

Thursday's child has far to go.

line from a traditional rhyme (compare qualities associated with birth on other days at entries under BEAUTY, GIFTS, SORROW, and WORK).

Travel broadens the mind.

English proverb, early 20th century.

The traveller discards his sense of shame.

people will behave in a strange country as they will not behave in their own; Japanese proverb.

Travelling is learning.

African proverb.

Treachery

Travelling is one way of lengthening life, at least in appearance.
American proverb, mid 20th century.

A wise man will climb Mount Fuji once, but only a fool will climb it twice.
Japanese proverb.

 # Treachery

See TRUST AND TREACHERY

Trees

The oak, the ash, and the elm may have particular attributes, but any tree can link the past with the future: Trees planted by the ancestors provide shade for their descendants.

The best time to plant a tree was twenty years ago. The second best is now.
even if you regret not having already planted a tree, it is still worth doing so; modern saying.

Beware of an oak, it draws the stroke; avoid an ash, it counts the flash; creep under the thorn, it can save you from harm.

recording traditional beliefs on where to shelter from lightning during a thunderstorm; English proverb, late 19th century.

Every elm has its man.

perhaps referring to the readiness of the tree to drop its branches on the unwary (elm wood was also traditionally used for coffins); English proverb, early 20th century.

In the woods it rains twice.

after a rainstorm, water continues to drip from overhead branches; German proverb.

One generation plants the trees; another sits in their shade.

Chinese proverb.

To plant a tree is to plant hope.

modern saying.

A seed hidden in the heart of an apple is an orchard invisible.

Welsh proverb; compare **All the flowers of tomorrow are in the seeds of today** at GARDENS.

Trust and Treachery

Trees planted by the ancestors provide shade for their descendants.

Chinese proverb; a comparable idea is found in the western classical world, in the writings of Caecilius Statius (d. after 166 BC) *Synephebi*, 'He plants the trees to serve another age.'

When the oak is before the ash, then you will only get a splash; When the ash is before the oak, then you will get a soak.

a traditional way of predicting whether the summer will be wet or dry on the basis of whether the oak or the ash is first to come into leaf in the spring; English proverb, mid 19th century.

※ Trust and Treachery

The traditional warning Promises, like piecrust, are made to be broken, *current since the 17th century, emphasizes the shrewdness of the Russian proverb,* Test before you trust.

Confidence is a plant of slow growth.

English proverb.

Fear the Greeks bearing gifts.

English proverb, late 19th century; originally from Virgil (70–19 BC) *Aeneid*, '*Equo ne credite, Teucri, Quidquid id est, timeo Danaos et dona ferentes* [Do not trust the horse,

Trojans. Whatever it is, I fear the Greeks even when they
bring gifts.]'

**Please to remember the Fifth of November,
Gunpowder Treason and Plot.
We know no reason why gunpowder treason Should
ever be forgot.**
traditional rhyme on the Gunpowder Plot (1605).

Promises, like piecrust, are made to be broken.
English proverb, late 17th century.

Test before you trust.
Russian proverb.

Would you buy a used car from this man?
campaign slogan directed against Richard Nixon.

**You cannot run with the hare and hunt with
the hounds.**
you must take one of two opposing sides; English proverb,
mid 15th century.

Truth

See also HONESTY, LIES

Telling the truth is an obligation (Tell the truth and
shame the devil), *but an admixture of tact may be*

Truth

advisable: When you shoot an arrow of truth, dip its point in honey.

Believe it or not.
title of syndicated newspaper feature (from 1918), written by Robert L. Ripley.

Fact is stranger than fiction.
English proverb, mid 19th century; compare **Truth is stranger than fiction** below.

Many a true word is spoken in jest.
an apparent joke may often include a shrewd comment, or what is spoken of as unlikely or improbable may in the future turn out to be true; English proverb, late 14th century.

An old error is always more popular than a new truth.
German proverb.

Se non è vero, è molto ben trovato.
Italian, 'If it is not true, it is a happy invention'; common saying from the 16th century.

Tell the truth and shame the devil.
by telling the truth one is taking the right course however embarrassing or difficult it may be; English proverb, mid 16th century; compare **Truth makes the Devil blush** below.

Truth is stranger than fiction.

implying that no invention can be as remarkable as what may actually happen; English proverb, early 19th century, from Byron *Don Juan* (1819–24), ''Tis strange—but true; for truth is always strange; Stranger than fiction'; compare **Fact is stranger than fiction** above.

Truth lies at the bottom of a well.

sometimes used to imply that the truth of a situation can be hard to find; English proverb, mid 16th century.

Truth makes the Devil blush.

English proverb, mid 20th century; compare **Tell the truth and shame the devil** above.

Truth will out.

in the end what has really happened will become apparent; English proverb, mid 15th century.

What everybody says must be true.

sometimes used ironically to assert that popular gossip is often inaccurate; English proverb, late 14th century.

When you shoot an arrow of truth, dip its point in honey.

advocating tact; Arab proverb.

Value

A sense of values is worth having: If you pay peanuts, you get monkeys, *and conversely* Gold may be bought too dear.

Everything has a price, but jade is priceless.

modern saying said to derive from a Chinese proverb extolling the value of jade.

Gold may be bought too dear.

wealth may be acquired at too great a price; English proverb, mid 16th century.

I am not rich enough to buy cheap goods.

a warning against practising false economies; modern saying.

If you pay peanuts, you get monkeys.

a poor rate of pay will attract only poorly qualified and incompetent staff (*peanuts* here means 'a small sum of money'); English proverb, mid 20th century.

It is a poor dog that's not worth whistling for.

a dog is of no value if the owner will not even go to the trouble of whistling for it; English proverb, mid 16th century.

Little things please little minds.

English proverb, late 16th century.

Nothing comes from nothing.

English proverb, late 14th century.

Nothing for nothing.

summarizing the attitude that nothing will be offered unless a return is assured; English proverb, early 18th century.

What can a monkey know of the taste of ginger?

ginger as the type of a rare and expensive delicacy; Indian proverb.

The worth of a thing is what it will bring.

the real value of something can only be measured by what another person is willing to pay for it; English proverb, mid 16th century.

Virtue

See also GOOD AND EVIL

Virtue should be pursued for its own sake (Virtue is its own reward), *although it will not necessarily evoke gratitude in others:* No good deed goes unpunished.

The good die young.

English proverb, late 17th century, often used ironically; compare **Whom the gods love die young** at YOUTH.

Good men are scarce.

English proverb, early 17th century.

Virtue

He lives long who lives well.

the reputation derived from living a good and moral life
will mean that one's name will last; English proverb, mid
16th century.

No good deed goes unpunished.

modern humorous saying, sometimes attributed to Oscar
Wilde but not traced in his writings.

See no evil, hear no evil, speak no evil.

conventionally represented by 'the three wise monkeys'
covering their eyes, ears, and mouth respectively with their
hands, and used particularly to imply a deliberate refusal to
notice something that is wrong; English proverb, early
20th century.

Virtue is its own reward.

the satisfaction of knowing that one has observed
appropriate moral standards should be all that is sought;
English proverb, early 16th century.

Warfare

See also THE ARMED FORCES, PEACE

War is seen as likely to cause more than physical injury and death: When war is declared, Truth is the first casualty.

A bayonet is a weapon with a worker at each end.
British pacifist slogan, 1940.

A bigger bang for a bigger buck.
Charles E. Wilson's defence policy, in *Newsweek* 22 March 1954.

Remember the Alamo!
Texan battle-cry at the battle of San Jacinto, 1836, referring to the defence of a Franciscan mission in the Texan War of Independence, in which all of the defenders were killed.

War is God's way of teaching Americans geography.
modern saying, widely attributed to the American writer Ambrose Bierce (1842–*c*.1914), but not found before the 1950s.

War will cease when men refuse to fight.
pacifist slogan, from *c*.1936, often in the form 'Wars will cease when…'

Ways and Means

When war is declared, Truth is the first casualty.
epigraph to Arthur Ponsonby's *Falsehood in Wartime*
(1928), perhaps deriving from Samuel Johnson in *The Idler*
11 November 1758, 'Among the calamities of war may be
jointly numbered the diminution of the love of truth, by the
falsehoods which interest dictates and credulity encourages';
attributed also to Hiram Johnson, speaking in the US
Senate, 1918, but not recorded in his speech.

❈ Ways and Means

When choosing the right tool (Honey catches more
flies than vinegar), *it is as well to be aware of what is
really essential:* It hardly matters if it is a white cat or a
black cat that catches the mice.

Catching's before hanging.
an essential step must be taken before the consequences can
ensue; English proverb, early 19th century.

Eat the mangoes. Do not count the trees.
concentrate on the task in hand; Indian proverb.

The end justifies the means.
English proverb, late 16th century.

Even if the sky falls down, there is a hole to escape.
there is often a way out of disaster; modern saying, said to
be a Korean proverb.

Fight fire with fire.

one should counter like with like; English proverb, mid 19th century.

Fire is a good servant, but a bad master.

acknowledging that fire is both essential for living and potentially destructive; English proverb, early 17th century.

First catch your hare.

referring to the first essential step that must be taken before a process can begin; English proverb, early 19th century, often attributed to the English cook Hannah Glasse (fl. 1747), but her directions for making hare soup are, 'Take your hare when it is cased' (*cased* here meaning 'skinned').

Give a man enough rope, and he will hang himself.

often used to mean that someone given enough licence or freedom will defeat themselves through their own mistakes; English proverb, mid 17th century.

The hammer shatters glass, but forges steel.

modern saying, said to be of Russian origin.

Honey catches more flies than vinegar.

soft or ingratiating words achieve more than sharpness; English proverb, mid 17th century.

If you can't beat them, join them.

often used in consolation or resignation; English proverb, mid 20th century.

Ways and Means

It hardly matters if it is a white cat or a black cat that catches the mice.
Chinese proverb.

It is good to make a bridge of gold to a flying enemy.
it is wiser to give passage to an enemy in flight, who may be desperate, than to bring them to bay; English proverb, late 16th century.

An old poacher makes the best gamekeeper.
someone who has formerly taken part in wrongdoing knows best how to counter it in others; English proverb, late 14th century.

One size does not fit all.
an assertion of individual requirements; earlier versions are based on the metaphor of different size shoes for different feet; English proverb, early 17th century.

The paths are many, but the goal is the same.
Indian proverb, deriving from Sanskrit.

The pen is mightier than the sword.
written words may often have more lasting force than military strength; English proverb, mid 17th century; compare **What is written with a pen cannot be cut out with an axe** at WRITING.

Set a thief to catch a thief.

used to imply that the person best placed to catch someone out in dishonest practices is one whose own nature tends that way; English proverb, mid 17th century.

A short cut is often a wrong cut.

a warning against trying to cut corners; Danish proverb.

There are more ways of killing a cat than choking it with cream.

there are more ways of achieving an end than giving an opponent a glut of what they most want; English proverb, mid 19th century.

There are more ways of killing a dog than choking it with butter.

there are more ways of achieving an end than giving an opponent a glut of what they most want; English proverb, mid 19th century.

There are more ways of killing a dog than hanging it.

there are more ways than one of achieving an end; English proverb, late 17th century.

There is more than one way to skin a cat.

English proverb, mid 19th century.

Weakness

There is nothing like leather.
referring to the toughness and durability of leather (the saying comes from one of Aesop's fables, in which a leatherworker contributed this opinion to a discussion on how to fortify a city); English proverb, late 17th century.

What matters is what works.
late 20th-century saying.

Weakness
See STRENGTH AND WEAKNESS

Wealth
See also MONEY, THRIFT

Possession of wealth confers status (Money makes a man), *and may be self-renewing:* Money makes money.

A diamond is forever.
advertising slogan for De Beers Consolidated Mines, 1940s onwards.

Few have too much, and fewer too little.
too much wealth is not necessarily a good thing; Danish proverb.

**If you really want to make a million, found a
new religion.**

previously attributed to L. Ron Hubbard (1911–86) in
B. Corydon and L. Ron Hubbard Jr. *L. Ron Hubbard* (1987),
but attribution subsequently rejected by L. Ron Hubbard Jr.,
who also dissociated himself from this book.

Money makes a man.

possession of wealth confers status; English proverb, early
16th century.

Money makes money.

implying that those who are already wealthy are likely to
become more so; English proverb, late 16th century.

Never ask about the first million.

modern saying, popularly associated with the very rich in
former Soviet bloc countries.

**The rich man gets his ice in the summer, and the
poor man gets his in the winter.**

contrasting luxury with hardship through apparent equality;
English proverb, early 20th century.

The Weather

*Traditional sayings about weather are likely to be
predictive* (North wind doth blow, we shall have snow,
Rain before seven, fine before eleven), *but a more*

The Weather

modern saying focuses on how to respond to such changes: There is no such thing as bad weather, only the wrong clothes.

As the day lengthens, so the cold strengthens.
recording the tradition that the coldest weather arrives when days begin to grow lighter; English proverb, early 17th century.

Clear moon, frost soon.
a clear night sky in winter may be a precursor of frost; traditional rhyme recorded from the 19th century.

Green Christmas, white Easter.
mild weather at Christmas may mean snow at Easter; German proverb.

Long foretold, long last; short notice, soon past.
if there is a long gap between the signs that the weather will change and the change itself, then the predicted weather will last a long time. If the intervening period is a short one, then the predicted weather will be of correspondingly short duration; English proverb, mid 19th century.

Nine months of winter and three months of hell.
on the long cold winters and hot summers supposedly typical of the Castilian climate; Spanish saying.

The Weather

North wind doth blow, we shall have snow.

traditional weather rhyme, deriving from a nursery rhyme of the early 19th century.

Rain before seven, fine before eleven.

English proverb, mid 19th century.

Rain, rain, go away, come again another day.

traditional rhyme, mid 17th century.

Red sky at night, shepherd's delight, Red sky in the morning, shepherd's warning.

good and bad weather respectively is presaged by a red sky at sunset and dawn; English proverb, late 14th century.

Robin Hood could brave all weathers but a thaw wind.

a *thaw wind* is a cold wind which accompanies the breaking up of frost; English proverb, mid 19th century.

So much sun as shines on Shrove Tuesday, so it shines all Lent.

traditional prediction.

There is no such thing as bad weather, only the wrong clothes.

late 20th-century saying.

Weddings

A warm January, a cold May.
mild weather in January means there will be cold weather in May; Welsh proverb.

When the stars begin to huddle, the earth will soon become a puddle.
when cloud cover begins to thicken (threatening rain), groups of stars still visible appear to huddle together; traditional rhyme recorded from the 19th century.

When the wind is in the east, 'tis good for neither man nor beast.
referring to the traditional bitterness of the east wind; English proverb, early 17th century.

Winter thunder, summer hunger.
thunderstorms in winter are taken as presage of a poor harvest; English proverb.

✲ Weddings

See also MARRIAGE

The day chosen for one's wedding may turn out to be important: Marry in May, rue for aye, *but* Happy is the bride the sun shines on.

Always a bridesmaid, never a bride.

recording the belief that to be a bridesmaid too often is
unlucky for one's own chances of marriage; English proverb,
late 19th century.

Happy is the bride the sun shines on.

English proverb, mid 17th century.

Marry in May, rue for aye.

English proverb, late 17th century.

**Now you will feel no rain, for each of you will be
shelter for the other. Now you will feel no cold, for
each of you will be warmth for the other.**

from the saying known as the 'Apache Blessing'.

One wedding brings another.

English proverb, mid 17th century.

Winning and Losing

See also SUCCESS AND FAILURE

*There is a consensus that winning and losing are both a
part of the pattern of life:* What you lose on the swings,
you gain on the roundabouts.

Heads I win, tails you lose.

I win in any event; *heads* and *tails* the obverse and reverse
images on a coin; English proverb, late 17th century.

Winter

What you lose on the swings, you gain on the roundabouts.

One's losses and gains tend to cancel one another out; English proverb, early 20th century.

A winner never quits, and a quitter never wins.

American proverb, early 20th century.

You can't win them all.

used as an expression of consolation or resignation; English proverb, mid 20th century.

 # Winter

See also AUTUMN, SPRING, SUMMER, THE WEATHER

Sayings about winter reflect both weather lore (February fill dyke, be it black or white), *and traditional activities for the season:* On Saint Thomas the Divine, kill all turkeys, geese and swine.

Candlemas day, put beans in the clay, put candles and candlesticks away.

recording the tradition that the feast of Candlemas, on 2 February, was the time for planting beans; English proverb, late 17th century.

February fill dyke, be it black or white.
February is a month likely to bring rain (black) or snow
(white); English proverb, mid 16th century.

The fire is winter's fruit.
Arabic proverb.

**If Candlemas day be sunny and bright, winter will
have another flight; if Candlemas day be cloudy
with rain, winter is gone and won't come again.**
English proverb, late 17th century.

**If in February there be no rain, 'tis neither good for
hay nor grain.**
a drought in February will be damaging to crops later in the
year; English proverb, early 18th century.

**If Saint Paul's day be fair and clear, it will betide a
happy year.**
the feast of the conversion of St Paul is 25 January; English
proverb, late 16th century.

**On Saint Thomas the Divine kill all turkeys, geese
and swine.**
21 December, the traditional feast-day in the Western
Church of St Thomas the Apostle, taken as marking the
season at which domestic animals not kept through the
winter were to be slaughtered; English proverb, mid
18th century.

Wisdom

The winter does not go without looking backward.
there is likely to be bad weather towards the end of winter;
Finnish proverb.

**Winter either bites with its teeth or lashes
with its tail.**
bad weather is expected at either the beginning or the end
of winter; Montenegrin proverb.

Winter is summer's heir.
the warmth of summer naturally gives way to the cold of
winter; English proverb.

Winter never rots in the sky.
the arrival of winter is not delayed; English proverb, early
17th century.

 # Wisdom

Wisdom may be found in unexpected places.

Fools ask questions that wise men cannot answer.
a foolish person may put a question to which there is no
simple or easily given answer; English proverb, mid
17th century.

**A little nonsense now and then, is relished by the
wisest men.**
American proverb, early 20th century.

Out of the mouths of babes —.

young children may sometimes speak with disconcerting
wisdom; English proverb, late 19th century, with allusion to
the Bible (Psalms), 'Out of the mouth of very babes and
sucklings hast thou ordained strength, because of
thine enemies.'

Women

See also MEN AND WOMEN

Traditional views on what is appropriate for women
(A whistling woman and a crowing hen, is good for
neither God nor men) *contrast with more radical
assessments of a woman's place in the world:* Women
hold up half the sky.

Burn your bra.

feminist slogan, 1970s.

Far-fetched and dear-bought is good for ladies.

expensive or exotic articles are suitable for women; English
proverb, mid 14th century.

The female of the species is more deadly than the male.

English proverb, early 20th century, from the title of a poem
(1919) by Rudyard Kipling.

Women

The hand that rocks the cradle rules the world.
referring to the strength of a woman's indirect influence on the male world; English proverb, mid 19th century.

Hell hath no fury like a woman scorned.
a woman whose love has turned to hate is the most savage of creatures; a fury here may be either one of the avenging deities of classical mythology, or more generally someone in a state of frenzied rage; English proverb, late 17th century.

Long and lazy, little and loud; fat and fulsome, pretty and proud.
categorizing supposed physical and temperamental characteristics in women; English proverb, late 16th century.

Silence is a woman's best garment.
often used as recommending a traditionally submissive and discreet role for women; English proverb, mid 16th century.

Votes for women.
slogan of the women's suffrage movement, adopted when it proved impossible to use a banner with the longer slogan 'Will the Liberal Party Give Votes for Women?' made by Emmeline Pankhurst, Christabel Pankhurst, and Annie Kenney.

A whistling woman and a crowing hen are neither fit for God nor men.

both the woman and the hen are considered unnatural, and therefore unlucky; English proverb, early 18th century.

A woman, a dog, and a walnut tree, the more you beat them the better they be.

the walnut tree was beaten firstly to bring down the fruit, and then to break down long shoots and encourage short fruit-bearing ones; English proverb, late 16th century.

A woman and a ship ever want mending.

both women and ships require constant attention and expenditure; English proverb, late 16th century.

A woman's place is in the home.

reflecting the traditional view of a woman's role; English proverb, mid 19th century.

Women hold up half the sky.

women should be considered equal in status to men; Chinese proverb.

Words ❀

See also NAMES, SAYINGS, SPEECH, WORDS AND DEEDS, WRITING

There are contrasting views on the power of a word: we are told that The swiftest horse cannot overtake the word once spoken, *but on the other hand,* Hard words break no bones.

All words are pegs to hang ideas on.
American proverb, late 19th century.

Elephants are contagious.
Surrealist 'proverb'.

Hard words break no bones.
the damage done by verbal attack is limited; English proverb, late 17th century.

I before e, except after c.
traditional spelling rule, 19th century.

If you take hyphens seriously you will go mad.
said to be from a style book in use with Oxford University Press, New York; perhaps apocryphal.

The quick brown fox jumps over the lazy dog.
traditional sentence used by keyboarders to ensure that all letters of the alphabet are functioning.

Sticks and stones may break my bones, but words will never hurt me.
verbal attack does no real injury; English proverb, late 19th century.

The swiftest horse cannot overtake the word once spoken.

Chinese proverb; compare Horace (65–8) *Epistles*, 'And once sent out, a word takes wing beyond recall.'

Words and Deeds

See also ACTION AND INACTION, WORDS

There is a consensus in favour of action (Example is better than precept), *but we are warned that it is also wise to keep a guard on the tongue:* Don't add insult to injury.

Actions speak louder than words.

real feeling is expressed not by what someone says but by what they do; English proverb, early 17th century.

Brag is a good dog, but Holdfast is better.

perseverance is a better quality than ostentation; English proverb, early 18th century.

Don't add insult to injury.

recommendation not to treat a person one has hurt with contempt as well; American proverb, mid 18th century.

Example is better than precept.

English proverb, early 15th century.

Words and Deeds

Fine words butter no parsnips.
nothing is ever achieved by fine words alone (*butter* was
the traditional garnish for parsnips); English proverb,
mid 17th century.

**It is not the same thing to talk of bulls as to be in
the bullring.**
Spanish saying.

One picture is worth ten thousand words.
English proverb, early 20th century.

An ounce of practice is worth a pound of precept.
a small amount of practical assistance is worth more than a
great deal of advice; English proverb, late 16th century.

Philosophy bakes no bread.
traditional criticism of philosophy as lacking practical
application, recorded from the 19th century.

Practise what you preach.
you should follow the advice you give to others; English
proverb, late 14th century.

Stabs heal, but bad words never.
words can inflict more lasting wounds than any physical
hurt; Spanish proverb.

Talk is cheap.

it is easier to say than to do something; English proverb, mid 19th century.

Talk will not cook rice.

modern saying, said to be a Chinese proverb.

Threatened men live long.

threats are often not put into effect, and those who express resentment are actually much less dangerous than those who conceal animosity; English proverb, mid 16th century.

The tongue is like a sharp knife, it can kill without drawing blood.

Chinese saying.

Vision without action is a daydream, Action without vision is a nightmare.

recommending a balance between idealism and reality; modern saying, said to derive from a Japanese proverb.

Words are sweet, but they never take the place of food.

African proverb.

Work

See also EMPLOYMENT, IDLENESS, LEISURE

Industry is traditionally commended (Practice makes perfect), *but it should be properly rewarded:* The labourer is worthy of his hire.

Arbeit macht frei.

German, 'Work liberates', words inscribed on the gates of Dachau concentration camp, 1933, and subsequently on those of Auschwitz.

The better the day, the better the deed.

frequently used to justify working on a Sunday or Holy Day; English proverb, early 17th century.

Every man to his trade.

one should operate within one's own area of expertise; English proverb, late 16th century.

Fools and bairns should never see half-done work.

the unwise and the inexperienced may judge the quality of a finished article from its rough unfinished state; English proverb, early 18th century.

From beavers, bees should learn to mend their ways. A bee works; a beaver works and plays.

American proverb, mid 20th century.

The labourer is worthy of his hire.

someone should be properly recompensed for effort;
English proverb, late 14th century, from the Bible
(Luke 10:7).

Like master, like man.

English proverb, mid 16th century; *man* here
means 'servant'.

One volunteer is worth two pressed men.

a *pressed man* was someone forcibly enlisted by the press
gang, a body of men which in the 18th and 19th centuries
was employed to enlist men forcibly into service in the army
or navy; English proverb, early 18th century.

Practice makes perfect.

often used as an encouragement; English proverb, mid
16th century.

Root, hog, or die.

advocating hard work and independence; *root* (of an
animal), turn up the ground with its snout in search of food;
American proverb, early 19th century.

Saturday's child works hard for a living.

first line of a traditional rhyme, mid 19th century (compare
qualities associated with birth on other days at entries under
BEAUTY, GIFTS, SORROW, and TRAVEL).

Work

A short horse is soon curried.
a slight task is soon completed (literally, that it does not take long to rub down a short horse with a curry-comb); English proverb, mid 14th century.

Too many cooks spoil the broth.
the involvement of too many people is likely to mean that something is done badly; English proverb, late 16th century.

Trifles make perfection, but perfection is no trifle.
American proverb, mid 20th century, from a comment attributed to the painter Michelangelo (1475–1564).

Two boys are half a boy, and three boys are no boy at all.
the more boys there are present, the less work will be done; English proverb, mid 20th century.

Where bees are, there is honey.
industrious work is necessary to create riches; English proverb, early 17th century.

Work expands so as to fill the time available.
English proverb, mid 20th century, from C. Northcote Parkinson *Parkinson's Law* (1958), 'Work expands so as to fill the time available for its completion.'

Worry

Worry is not only exhausting (Care killed the cat,
It is not work that kills, but worry), *but ultimately
pointless:* Worry is like a rocking chair: both give you
something to do, but neither get you anywhere.

Care killed the cat.
the meaning of *care* has shifted somewhat from 'worry,
grief' to 'care, caution'; English proverb, late 16th century.

Do not meet troubles half way.
warning against anxiety about something that has not yet
happened; English proverb, late 19th century.

It is not work that kills, but worry.
direct effort is less stressful than constant concern; English
proverb, late 19th century.

Sufficient unto the day is the evil thereof.
dealing with unpleasant matters should be left until it
becomes necessary; English proverb, mid 18th century, with
allusion to the Bible (Matthew 6:34).

Worry is interest paid on trouble before it falls due.
American proverb, early 20th century.

Worry is like a rocking chair: both give you
something to do, but neither gets you anywhere.
American proverb, mid 20th century.

Worry often gives a small thing a big shadow.
Swedish proverb.

 # Writing

See also BOOKS, WORDS

Not only is writing powerful (What is written with a pen cannot be cut out with an axe), *it is likely to reveal the essential nature of the writer:* Writing is a picture of the writer's heart.

The art of writing is the art of applying the seat of the pants to the seat of the chair.
American proverb, mid 20th century.

For most of history, Anonymous was a woman.
modern saying, mid 20th century, often associated with the English writer Virginia Woolf (1882–1941).

He who would write and can't write can surely review.
American proverb, mid 19th century.

Paper bleeds little.
Spanish proverb.

Paper is patient.
paper allows the writer to put down what they choose; German proverb.

What is written with a pen cannot be cut out with an axe.

words are more powerful than violence; Russian proverb; compare **The pen is mightier than the sword** at

WAYS AND MEANS.

Writing is a picture of the writer's heart.

Chinese proverb.

Youth

See also AGE, CHILDREN

To be young is often to overestimate one's powers
(Young folks think old folks to be fools, but old folks
know young folks to be fools), *but even the
irresponsible young may grow up to more serious ways:*
Wanton kittens make sober cats.

All dancing girls are nineteen years old.
Japanese proverb.

Never send a boy to do a man's job.
someone who is young and inexperienced should not be
given too much responsibility; English proverb, mid
20th century.

The old net is cast aside while the new net goes fishing.
the future belongs to the young; Maori proverb.

Soon ripe, soon rotten.
a warning against precocity, meaning that notably early
achievement is unlikely to be long-lasting; English proverb,
late 14th century (earlier in Latin).

Wanton kittens make sober cats.

someone who in youth is light-minded and lascivious
may be soberly behaved in later life; English proverb,
early 18th century.

Whom the gods love die young.

the happiest fate is to die before health and strength are lost;
English proverb, mid 16th century; the idea is found in the
classical world in Menander (342–*c.*292 BC) *Dis Exapaton*,
'Whom the gods love dies young'; compare also **The good
die young** at VIRTUE.

**Young folks think old folks to be fools, but old folks
know young folks to be fools.**

asserting the value of the experience of life which comes
with age over youth and inexperience; English proverb, late
16th century.

Youth must be served.

Some indulgence should be given to the wishes and
enthusiasms of youth; English proverb, early 19th century.

Keyword Index ✵

Each context line represents the opening words of a proverb (initial 'a' and 'the' being omitted). The proverb will be found in alphabetical sequence in the given section.

Keyword Index

Keyword Index

Keyword Index

Keyword Index

Keyword Index

Keyword Index

Keyword Index

Keyword Index

Keyword Index

Keyword Index

Keyword Index

Keyword Index

Keyword Index

Keyword Index

Keyword Index

door creaking door hangs
  longest SICKNESS
  door must be either shut or
  open CHOICE
  golden key can open any
  door CORRUPTION
  postern door makes a
  thief OPPORTUNITY
  Teachers open the
  door EDUCATION
  When one door shuts, another
  opens OPPORTUNITY
  When poverty comes in at
  the door POVERTY
dose dose of adversity is
  often ADVERSITY
double Shared joy is double
  joy SYMPATHY
doubt When in doubt, do
  nowt ACTION AND INACTION
dough Drive for show, and
  putt for dough SPORTS
  AND GAMES
down Up like a rocket, down like
  a stick SUCCESS AND FAILURE
  What goes up must come
  down FATE
dragons Dragons beget
  dragons FAMILY
  Here be dragons INVENTIONS
  AND DISCOVERIES
drama We won't make a drama
  out of CAUTION
draw good painter can draw a
  devil ART
draws Whosoever draws his
  sword against REVOLUTION AND
  REBELLION
dreaders Evil doers are evil
  dreaders CONSCIENCE
dream Dream of a
  funeral DREAMS
  peace is the dream of the

wise PEACE
  To dream of the dead is a sign
  of rain DREAMS
  You cannot dream yourself
  into CHARACTER
dreaming Those who lose
  dreaming DREAMS
dreams Dreams go by
  contraries DREAMS
  Dreams retain the infirmities
  of DREAMS
  God sleeps in the stone,
  dreams HUMAN RACE
  Morning dreams come
  true DREAMS
dress Dress for the job you
  want DRESS
drink Don't ask a man to drink
  and drive DRINK
  drunkard's cure is drink
  again DRUNKENNESS
  Eat, drink and be merry, for
  tomorrow LIFESTYLES
  When you drink water,
  remember GRATITUDE
drinking When drinking water,
  remember the PARENTS
drinks He that drinks beer, thinks
  beer DRUNKENNESS
dripping dripping June sets all in
  tune SUMMER
drive Don't ask a man to drink
  and drive DRINK
  Drive for show, and putt for
  dough SPORTS AND GAMES
drives Needs must when the devil
  drives NECESSITY
  One nail drives out another
  SIMILARITY AND DIFFERENCE
drop last drop makes the cup run
  over EXCESS
dropping Constant dropping
  wears away DETERMINATION

Keyword Index

Keyword Index

Keyword Index

Keyword Index

Keyword Index

Keyword Index

424

Keyword Index

pot boils, friendship
lives HOSPITALITY

frog child of a frog is a
frog FAMILY
frog in a well knows
nothing of SELF-ESTEEM AND
SELF-ASSERTION

frond As one fern frond dies,
another LEADERSHIP

frost Clear moon, frost
soon WEATHER

frosts So many mists in March, so
many frosts SPRING

fruit fire is winter's fruit WINTER
He that would eat fruit EFFORT
September blow soft till the
fruit's AUTUMN
stolen fruit are
sweet TEMPTATION
tree is known by its
fruit CHARACTER
When all fruit fails, welcome
haws NECESSITY

frying Keep one eye on the
frying-pan COOKING

Fuji wise man will climb Mount
Fuji once TRAVEL

full Full cup, steady
hand CAUTION
It's ill speaking between a
full man FOOD

fullness Out of the fullness of
the heart FEELINGS

fun Time flies when you're
having fun HAPPINESS

funeral Dream of a
funeral DREAMS
One funeral makes
many DEATH

furrow old horse does not spoil
the furrow AGE

further Go further and fare worse
SATISFACTION AND DISCONTENT

fury Hell hath no fury like a
woman scorned WOMEN

furze When the furze is in
bloom LOVE

future man's best reputation for
his future REPUTATION
There's no future like the
present FUTURE

gain No pain, no gain EFFORT
Nothing venture, nothing
gain THOROUGHNESS
One man's loss is another
man's gain CIRCUMSTANCE
AND SITUATION
There's no great loss without
some gain CIRCUMSTANCE AND
SITUATION

game After the game, the king
and the pawn EQUALITY
Lookers-on see most of the
game ACTION AND INACTION

gamekeeper old poacher makes
the best gamekeeper WAYS
AND MEANS

garbage Garbage in, garbage
out COMPUTING

garden book is like a
garden BOOKS
garden is never
finished GARDENS
More things grow in the
garden GARDENS
Select a proper site for your
garden GARDENS

gardener It is not enough for a
gardener FLOWERS

garment Silence is a woman's best
garment WOMEN

gather Drops that gather one by
one QUANTITIES AND QUALITIES

gaze Only the eagle can gaze at
the sun STRENGTH AND
WEAKNESS

Keyword Index

Keyword Index

Keyword Index

Keyword Index

Keyword Index

Keyword Index

Keyword Index

Keyword Index

Keyword Index

Keyword Index

Keyword Index

Keyword Index

Keyword Index

Keyword Index

Out of the mouths of
babes — WISDOM

moutons *Revenons à ces*
moutons DETERMINATION

move Did the earth move
for you SEX
When you pray, move your
feet RELIGION

moved shall not be
moved DETERMINATION

moves If it moves, salute
it ARMED FORCES

much Few have too much, and
fewer too little WEALTH
Much would have more GREED
Sow much, reap much CAUSES
AND CONSEQUENCES
You can have too much of a
good thing EXCESS

muck Where there's muck there's
brass MONEY

muckle Many a mickle
makes a muckle QUANTITIES
AND QUALITIES

mulberry With time and patience
the mulberry leaf PATIENCE

mule If you lead your mule to the
top PROBLEMS AND SOLUTIONS

multitude Charity covers a
multitude of sins FORGIVENESS

mummified Custom is
mummified by habit CUSTOM
AND HABIT

murder Killing no
murder MURDER
Murder will out MURDER

music Music helps not the
toothache MUSIC
When the music
changes CHANGE

must What must be, must be FATE

mustard After meat,
mustard EATING

nail For want of a nail the shoe
was lost PREPARATION AND
READINESS
nail that sticks up is certain
to MANAGEMENT
One nail drives out
another SIMILARITY AND
DIFFERENCE

name Change the name and not
the letter MARRIAGE
Give a dog a bad name and
hang GOSSIP
good name is better than a
golden girdle REPUTATION
He that has an ill
name REPUTATION
We name the guilty men GUILT

names No names, no
pack drill SECRECY

Naples See Naples and
die TOWNS AND CITIES

nation As Maine goes, so goes the
nation POLITICS
Nation shall speak peace
unto BROADCASTING
nation without a
language COUNTRIES AND
PEOPLES

national national debt, if it is not
excessive DEBT AND
BORROWING

nature Death is nature's
way DEATH
father is a banker provided by
nature PARENTS
Nature abhors a
vacuum NATURE
Self-preservation is the first law
of nature SELF-INTEREST
Some sleep five hours; nature
requires SLEEP
You can drive out nature with a
pitchfork NATURE

Keyword Index

Keyword Index

Keyword Index

Keyword Index

Keyword Index

Keyword Index

proverbs Proverbs are the coins of the people   SAYINGS

providence Providence is always on the side of   ARMED FORCES

public One does not wash one's dirty linen   SECRECY

publicity Any publicity is good publicity   ADVERTISING

pudding proof of the pudding is in the eating   HYPOTHESIS AND FACT

puddle sun loses nothing by shining into a puddle   GOOD AND EVIL

When the stars begin to huddle, the earth will soon become a puddle   WEATHER

punctuality Punctuality is the art of guessing   PUNCTUALITY

Punctuality is the politeness of princes   PUNCTUALITY

Punctuality is the soul of business   PUNCTUALITY

pungent older the ginger, the more pungent   AGE

Sour, sweet, bitter, pungent   FATE

pupil When the pupil is ready, the master   EDUCATION

purse You can't make a silk purse   FUTILITY

pursueth guilty flee when no man pursueth   GUILT

push Do not push the river, it will flow   FUTILITY

put Never put off till tomorrow   HASTE AND DELAY

putt Drive for show, and putt for dough   SPORTS AND GAMES

quality Every good quality is contained in ginger   HEALTH

Never mind the quality, feel the width   QUANTITIES AND QUALITIES

quarrel It takes two to make a quarrel   ARGUMENT

quarrel of lovers is the renewal   LOVE

quart You cannot get a quart into a pint   FUTILITY

queer There's nowt so queer as folk   HUMAN RACE

question Ask a silly question and you get   FOOLS

civil question deserves a civil answer   MANNERS

Fools ask questions that wise men   WISDOM

There are two sides to every question   JUSTICE

To question and ask is a moment's shame   THINKING

quick quick brown fox jumps over the lazy dog   WORDS

quickly He gives twice who gives quickly   GENEROSITY

Quickly come, quickly go   LOYALTY

quickness quickness of the hand deceives the eye   DECEPTION

quiet best doctors are Dr Quiet, Dr Diet   MEDICINE

quiet conscience sleeps in thunder   CONSCIENCE

quits winner never quits, and a quitter never wins   WINNING AND LOSING

quitter winner never quits, and a quitter never wins   WINNING AND LOSING

quote devil can quote Scripture   SAYINGS

race Pace makes the race   HORSES

Keyword Index

Keyword Index

roses Take time to smell the
roses   LEISURE
Time brings roses   PATIENCE
rots Winter never rots in the
sky   WINTER
rotten rotten apple injures its
neighbour   CORRUPTION
Small choice in rotten
apples   CHOICE
Soon ripe, soon rotten   YOUTH
round Love makes the world go
round   LOVE
row Call on God, but row
away   CAUTION
royal There is no royal road to
learning   EDUCATION
rudder Who won't be ruled by the
rudder   CAUSES AND
CONSEQUENCES
rudderless widow is a rudderless
boat   MARRIAGE
rue Marry in May, rue for
aye   WEDDINGS
rule Divide and
rule   GOVERNMENT
exception proves the
rule   HYPOTHESIS AND FACT
golden rule of life is   BEGINNING
Self-interest is the rule
SELF-INTEREST
There is an exception to every
rule   HYPOTHESIS AND FACT
ruled Who won't be ruled by the
rudder   CAUSES AND
CONSEQUENCES
rules hand that rocks the cradle
rules   WOMEN
Rules are made to be
broken   LAW
run All rivers run into the
sea   RIVERS
You cannot run with the
hare   TRUST AND TREACHERY

runs guilty one always
runs   GUILT
He that runs may
read   READING
He who fights and runs
away   CAUTION
Russian Scratch a Russian
and you find   COUNTRIES
AND PEOPLES
rust Better to wear out than to
rust   IDLENESS
rusts If gold rusts, what will iron
do   CORRUPTION
Sabbath child that is born on the
Sabbath   CHILDREN
sack You can't hide an awl in a
sack   SECRECY
sacks Empty sacks will never
stand upright   POVERTY
safe Better be safe than
sorry   CAUTION
Just when you thought it was
safe   DANGER
Safe bind, safe find   CAUTION
safety Caution is the parent of
safety   CAUTION
There is safety in
numbers   QUANTITIES AND
QUALITIES
said They haif said: Quhat say
they   DEFIANCE
What the soldier said isn't
evidence   GOSSIP
sailor One cannot become a good
sailor   EFFORT
sailors Heaven protects children,
sailors   DANGER
saint Devil was sick, the Devil a
saint   GRATITUDE
greater the sinner, the greater
the saint   GOOD AND EVIL
If Saint Paul's day be fair and
clear   WINTER

Keyword Index

Keyword Index

So much sun as shines
on   WEATHER

shining sun loses nothing by
shining into a puddle   GOOD
AND EVIL

ship Do not spoil the ship for a
ha'porth of tar   THOROUGHNESS
One hand for oneself and one
for the ship   SEA
woman and a ship ever want
mending   WOMEN

ships Loose lips sink
ships   GOSSIP

shirt Near is my shirt, but nearer
my skin   SELF-INTEREST

shirtsleeves From shirtsleeves to
shirtsleeves   SUCCESS AND
FAILURE

shoe For want of a nail the shoe
was lost   PREPARATION AND
READINESS
If the shoe fits,
wear it   NAMES

shoemaker shoemaker's son
always goes   FAMILY

shoes I cried because I had no
shoes   MISFORTUNES
It's ill waiting for dead men's
shoes   AMBITION
You need more than dancing
shoes   DANCE

shoot When you shoot an arrow
of truth   TRUTH

shop Keep your own
shop   BUSINESS

shopping Only — shopping days
to Christmas   CHRISTMAS

shore I sit on the shore, and wait
for the wind   PATIENCE

shoreline larger the shoreline of
knowledge   KNOWLEDGE

shorn God tempers the wind to
the shorn lamb   SYMPATHY

short Art is long and life is
short   LIFE
short cut is often a wrong
cut   WAYS AND MEANS
short horse is soon
curried   WORK
Short reckonings make
long friends   DEBT AND
BORROWING

shortest longest way home is the
shortest   PATIENCE

show Drive for show, and putt for
dough   SPORTS AND GAMES
show must go
on   DETERMINATION
Tell me and I'll forget. Show me
and   TEACHING

showers April showers bring
forth May flowers   SPRING

shrimp shrimp that falls
asleep   ACTION AND INACTION
When whales fight, the shrimp's
back is broken   POWER

shrouds Shrouds have no
pockets   MONEY

shut door must be either shut or
open   CHOICE
It's too late to shut the
stable door   FORESIGHT
shut mouth catches no
flies   SILENCE

shuts When one door shuts,
another opens   OPPORTUNITY

shy Once bitten, twice
shy   EXPERIENCE

sick Devil was sick, the Devil a
saint   GRATITUDE
Hope deferred makes the heart
sick   HOPE

sickly bloody war and a sickly
season   ARMED FORCES

side bread never falls but on its
buttered side   MISFORTUNES

Keyword Index

Keyword Index

Keyword Index

stolen Nothing is stolen without hands HONESTY
Stolen fruit are sweet TEMPTATION
Stolen waters are sweet TEMPTATION

stone God sleeps in the stone, dreams HUMAN RACE
Stone-dead hath no fellow DEATH
You cannot get blood from a stone FUTILITY

stones Cross the river by feeling the stones CAUTION
Sticks and stones may break my bones WORDS
You buy land, you buy stones BUYING AND SELLING

stools Between two stools one falls INDECISION

stoop He that will not stoop for a pin PRIDE

stopped Even a stopped clock is right twice a day TIME

storm After a storm comes a calm PEACE
Any port in a storm CRISES
sharper the storm, the sooner it's over OPTIMISM AND PESSIMISM

story everyday story of country folk COUNTRY AND THE TOWN
Every picture tells a story KNOWLEDGE
One story is good till another is told HYPOTHESIS AND FACT

stout Put a stout heart to a stey brae DETERMINATION

stove cook is no better than her stove COOKING

straight God writes straight with crooked lines GOD

No one was ever lost on a straight road PREPARATION AND READINESS

strain Don't strain at a gnat, and swallow BELIEF
Let the train take the strain TRAVEL

Strand You're never alone with a Strand SMOKING

strange Politics makes strange bedfellows POLITICS

stranger Fact is stranger than fiction TRUTH
tears of the stranger are only water SYMPATHY
Truth is stranger than fiction TRUTH

straw drowning man will clutch at a straw HOPE
It is the last straw EXCESS
straw vote only shows which way POLITICS
You cannot make bricks without straw FUTILITY

straws Straws tell which way the wind blows KNOWLEDGE

stream stream cannot rise above its source CHARACTER

strength Strength through joy STRENGTH AND WEAKNESS
Union is strength COOPERATION

stretch Stretch your arm no further than THRIFT

strike Strike while the iron is hot OPPORTUNITY

strikes Lightning never strikes twice CHANCE AND LUCK
Three strikes and you're out CRIME AND PUNISHMENT

striking It is a striking coincidence that COUNTRIES AND PEOPLES

Keyword Index

Keyword Index

Keyword Index

Keyword Index

Keyword Index

Keyword Index

490

Keyword Index

Keyword Index

Keyword Index

Keyword Index